International stu

series e

MW00914079

Rugby and the
South African nation

MANCHESTER
UNIVERSITY PRESS

Rugby and the
South African nation

**Sport, cultures, politics and power in
the old and new South Africas**

David R. Black
and John Nauright

MANCHESTER UNIVERSITY PRESS
Manchester and New York

Distributed exclusively in the USA by St. Martin's Press

Published by Manchester University Press
Oxford Road, Manchester M13 9NR, UK
and Room 400, 175 Fifth Avenue, New York, NY 10010, USA

Distributed exclusively in the USA by
St. Martin's Press, Inc., 175 Fifth Avenue, New York,
NY 10010, USA

Distributed exclusively in Canada by
UBC Press, University of British Columbia, 6344 Memorial Road,
Vancouver, BC, Canada V6T 1Z2

British Library Cataloguing-in-Publication Data
A catalogue record for this book is available from the British Library

Library of Congress Cataloguing-in-Publication Data
Black, David R., 1947–
    Rugby and the South African nation : sport, cultures, politics,
and power in the old and new South Africas / David R. Black and John
Nauright.
        p.   cm. – (International studies in the history of sport)
    Includes bibliographical references and index.
    ISBN 0 7190 4931 8 (hardback). – ISBN 0 7190 4932 6 (paperback)
    1. Rugby Football – Social aspects – South Africa.   2. Rugby
football – South Africa – History.   3. South Africa – Race relations.
4. Rugby football – Political aspects – South Africa.   I. Nauright,
John, 1962–   .   II. Title.   III. Series.
GV945.9.S6B53   1998
796.333'0968–dc21   98–20906

ISBN 0 7190 4931 8 hardback
       0 7190 4932 6 paperback

First published in 1998

05 04 03 02 01 00 99 98   10 9 8 7 6 5 4 3 2

Typeset in Palatino
by Servis Filmsetting Ltd, Manchester

Printed in Great Britain
by Bell & Bain Ltd, Glasgow

Contents

Series editor's foreword

Rugby and the South African Nation is the final volume in the series *International Studies in the History of Sport*. The series was launched in 1987 due to the vision, initiative and enterprise of Manchester University Press and it was the first exclusive history of sport series in the academic world. It has made a notable contribution to the history of sport – a contribution to be continued elsewhere within the broader framework of a multi-disciplinary series *Sport in the Global Society* published by Frank Cass.

Series volumes that should be singled out for special mention due to their world-wide acclaim are Stephen Jones, *Sport, Politics and the Working Class: Organised Labour and Sport in Inter-War Britain*, Patricia Vertinsky, *The Eternally Wounded Woman: Women, Doctors and Exercise in the Late Nineteenth Century* and John Lowerson, *Sport and The English Middle Classes 1870–1914*.

The first foreword by this editor expressed the hope, in the form of an ambition, that the series would reduce, if not eradicate, the academic myopia associated with sports studies. It can be safely asserted that due to the excellence of its contributors it has done just that.

Abbreviations

ANC	African National Congress
ARU	Australian Rugby Union
BCM	Black Consciousness Movement
CABTA	Citizens All Black Tour Association
CODESA	Convention for a Democratic South Africa
CSRU	City and Suburban Rugby Union
GNU	Government of National Unity
HNP	Herstigte Nasionale Party
ICC	International Cricket Council
IOC	International Olympic Committee
IRB	International Rugby Board
MCC	Marylebone Cricket Club
MDM	Mass Democratic Movement
NOCSA	National Olympic Committee of South Africa
NP	National Party
NSC/NOSC	National (Olympic and) Sports Congress/National Sports Council since inception of the GNU
NZRFU	New Zealand Rugby Football Union
PFP	Progressive Federal Party
RWC	Rugby World Cup
SACOS	South African Council of Sport
SACRFB	South African Coloured Rugby Football Board
SACU	South African Cricket Union
SANROC	South African Non-Racial Olympic Committee
SANZAR	South Africa New Zealand Australia Rugby Inc.
SARA	South African Rugby Association
SARB	South African Rugby Board
SARFF	South African Rugby Football Federation
SARFU	South African Rugby Football Union
SARU	South African Rugby Union
SASA	South African Sports Association
TRFU	Transvaal Rugby Football Union
UCBSA	United Cricket Board of South Africa
UDF	United Democratic Front
WPCRFU	Western Province Coloured Rugby Football Union
WPRFU	Western Province Rugby Football Union
WRC	World Rugby Corporation

Preface and acknowledgments

Rugby emerged during the segregation and apartheid periods of South African history to become the dominant sport among white South Africans, though it was played and watched by many in the mixed-race or Coloured community as well as Africans, especially in the Eastern Cape region. South Africa's ability to participate in international rugby suffered little by comparison with other sports or areas of popular culture in the period of cultural boycotts, as it only faced isolation from 1985 to 1992. Even during that period, a New Zealand rebel team toured South Africa in 1986 as did a World team in 1989 to mark the centenary of the South African Rugby Board, the controlling body of white rugby. South Africa was, however, excluded from the first two Rugby World Cups (RWC) in 1987 and 1991. After the release of Nelson Mandela and the unbanning of key opposition political organisations in February 1992, South Africa quickly returned to international rugby with New Zealand and then world champions Australia briefly touring in July of that year. South Africa was also named as host of the 1995 Rugby World Cup. The Cup, won by South Africa in dramatic fashion, ironically became the most significant trans-racial moment of national celebration in the New South Africa since the April 1994 all-race elections, even though rugby was the sport most connected with apartheid oppression. Indeed, the National Party government and Afrikaner elite that implemented apartheid and ruled the country from 1948 into the 1990s actively used rugby as an expression of the power of white South Africa.

Soon after the 1995 victory it became clear that the white administrators who still controlled the key positions in the new unified South African Rugby Football Union (SARFU) had little serious interest in the development of rugby in black communities. Many development programmes were little more than showpieces for the international community, though some facilities were built and clinics organised in poor areas. More common were arguments between the SARFU and provincial unions over who should pay for development activities and facilities. While some black players have begun to appear at elite levels, many clubs have disappeared as a result of a 'unity' which amounted to a takeover by white competitions, much like West Germany's takeover of East Germany.

The attitudes of many white officials were laid bare when racist comments by the national rugby coach were caught on tape in late 1996. The tape was made public and broadcast nationally. As a result of these and other controversies, in 1997 the African National Congress-led government of South Africa called for a full judicial inquiry into the running of rugby. It felt that the SARFU under its president Louis Luyt (pronounced 'late') was damaging the sport, using it for self-accumulation and hindering the emergence of progressive practices in rugby. In reaction, the SARFU sued the government, asserting that it had no legal right to 'interfere' in the operations of a private organisation. In March 1998, President Mandela was forced to testify in the High Court to legitimate the legality of the inquiry. In April the National Sports Congress, which oversees sporting activity in South Africa, threatened to re-impose an international boycott against South African rugby and to strip the SARFU of the right to select the national rugby team and thus use the Springbok emblem worn by those teams unless changes were made immediately, including the resignation of Luyt and the SARFU executive. Finally, in May 1998, Luyt resigned, thus narrowly averting new boycotts.

While this issue may be resolved, at least in the short term, prior to the publication of this book, it nevertheless demonstrates that rugby in South Africa, highly political in the development of white nationalism, segregation and apartheid, has remained politically charged in the post-apartheid era. There are, however, hopeful if limited signs of change. During April 1998, for example, the Golden Cats team in the Super 12 competition (largely made up of players from the Gauteng (Transvaal) provincial side) announced the selection of the first black African player to make a South African team in the competition. In addition, in 1997 Sean Plaatjies, pictured on the cover, became the first black player to captain an official South African national side as captain of the schools national team.

In this book we examine the historical development of rugby in South Africa and the various ideologies that have been and are still attached to it. Rugby has represented at different times and in differing places imperial connections, Afrikaner nationalism, Islamic masculinity and Coloured community identity, sporting identity and culture among the educated African elite, racism and, for a brief time in 1995, a new pan-South African national identification. We explore each of these roles, paying particular attention to the links between rugby and politics in South Africa during the twentieth century.

This project began when we were working on widely varying PhD topics in Canada during the early 1990s. We were drawn to the central yet under-studied role of rugby in nationalist politics in South Africa, as well as to the international implications of South African rugby, particularly in relation to New Zealand. We initially focused on the significance of the rugby relationship between these two dominant rugby-playing nations of the twentieth century. Increasingly, however, we were drawn to an analysis of the place of rugby in South Africa's politics and its diverse cultures. While our early collaborative work took place in Kingston, Ontario, Canada, most of the book was written at about as great a distance as is geographically possible on this planet between Brisbane, Queensland in Australia and Halifax, Nova Scotia in Canada. Thanks to the support of the University of Queensland, in the form of a New Staff Research Grant, and the Australian Research Council, John Nauright was able to travel to Nova Scotia in 1995 and to South Africa in 1994, 1995 and 1996. In addition, the University of Queensland provided John with a period of study leave in 1997 during which we were able to finish the manuscript in the Nova Scotian autumn. David Black is indebted to the (now defunct) Cooperative Security Competitions Programme of Canada's Department of Foreign Affairs and International Trade for supporting travel to South Africa in 1994 and 1995. He also wishes to thank the Centre for Foreign Policy Studies at Dalhousie University, and in particular Paulette Dunn, for assistance with computing and communications in the completion of this project; and the Department of Political Science at McGill University for providing space in which to complete the writing of the manuscript.

We have incurred many debts during our research and writing on South Africa over a number of years, especially from the incredibly generous people of South Africa. We would like to thank several South Africans in particular, but acknowledge the assistance of many others. We especially thank Tim and Rose Clynick, Denise and John Jones, Andre Odendaal, Christopher Merrett, Albert Grundlingh, Peter and Louise Vale, Sue Parnell and Owen Crankshaw, John Baxter, Denver Hendricks, Ngconde Balfour, 'Meneer' Effendi, Goosain, Gassan and Fatima Emeran and their family and friends in the Bo-Kaap, Floris van der Merwe, Paul Dobson, Charlie Mather, Cecile Badenhorst, Herman Abrahams, Steve Strijdom, Hussein Solomon, Xavier Carim, and Sulona Reddy. Some background material in the second and third chapters is derived from collaborative work on South African cricket between John Nauright and Christopher Merrett which appears in full form as a chapter in Brian Stoddart and Keith Sandiford (eds), *The imperial game*, published by Manchester University Press in 1998.

Elsewhere, we would like to acknowledge the support and encouragement of Larry Swatuk, Audie Klotz, Tim Shaw, Jane Parpart, Alan Jeeves and the late Don Macintosh, an inspiration to a great many of us who have worked on issues of sport and politics. Thanks also to our editors at Manchester University Press for their patience, meticulousness and encouragement: Carolyn Hand, Vanessa Graham, Gemma Marren and Rachel Armstrong. Special thanks goes to Tara Magdalinski who provided the index and read many sections of the manuscript.

Finally, we would like to thank Heather and Tara for their loving support and encouragement over the years. We dedicate this book to them.

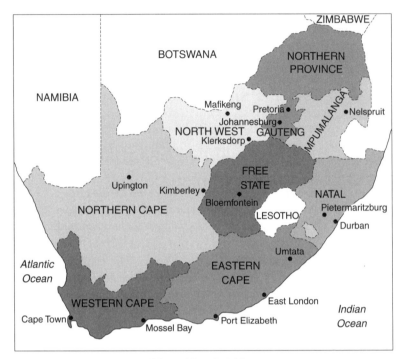

Map of South Africa

Chapter 1
Sport, culture, and politics

There are few national societies in which the cultural significance, indeed centrality, of sport has been more readily apparent than South Africa. Rugby in particular has held a position of extraordinary prominence and symbolic importance for the white South Africans who dominated the society during the development and entrenchment of modern sporting structures. While sport has been tied to power in South Africa, such links are far from unique. Where South Africa varied from other 'Western' countries in the post-World War Two era was in attaching social and cultural meanings to sport that were linked to official racist ideologies and policies. However, the importance of sport as a dominant popular cultural practice is a world-wide phenomenon, despite interesting variations in intensity and character. Rather more elusive are substantial conclusions regarding the political role and significance of dominant sporting practices, both within and across particular communities.[1]

It is to the elusive yet often influential role of sport in national, international and transnational politics that we first turn our attention. In what follows, we tackle the untenable yet resilient myth of sport existing above, beyond or beneath politics. The persistent attempts by state and corporate elites to use sport in a direct, instrumental fashion, with varying degrees of success, are discussed. More importantly, perhaps, we consider the pervasive and longer-term role of sport in political socialisation – particularly in forging national identities. Several major alternative theoretical approaches to conceptualising the role of sport in politics are compared. Finally, the significance of sport as a weapon of the weak – of critical (or counter-hegemonic) social organisations and movements both within and across national societies – is noted, as a prelude to our consideration of the place of rugby in the politics of South Africa. We argue that, although sport has most often served as a conservative and status quo oriented influence, submerging differences and making many society members (particularly males) feel good about their community, it can also serve as a powerful force for social change, particularly when these very qualities are attacked. Because of its immense popularity, it has the capacity to puncture the popular imagination, and contribute importantly to processes of re-socialisation and change – albeit in an indirect and long-term fashion. It is these capacities – both conservative and progressive – that we see as being brought to bear in the context of the South African rugby cultures, with important political repercussions.

The resilient myth of separate spheres

As has been widely noted, it is no longer possible for any serious social commentator to posit a separation between the worlds of sport and politics.[2] Yet the notion that sport is, or should be, separate from politics – what Allison has referred to as the myth of autonomy – has demonstrated impressive resilience. There have been a number of sources of this myth. Historically, it was deeply embedded in British sporting ideology, with its celebration of the ideal of amateurism, and carried forward by the Olympic movement during the long tenure of Avery Brundage (notably, it has been much weaker beyond the Anglo-Saxon world). More recently, this myth has been supported both by those who view sport as play – a pleasurable recreation but ultimately socially and politically trivial – and those who maintain an exaggerated sense of the nobility and purity of sport and the athlete, untainted by the sordid world of the political. In other words, it has been widely seen as either below or above politics.[3] The tenaciousness of the myth of autonomy has been particularly marked in the academic world, where sociologists, historians and above all political scientists interested in sport have only since the early 1980s begun to win acceptance of their research pursuits as serious. In practice, it is clear that many people who have little interest in politics are passionate sports participants or (more typically) fans, while many radical critics of the role of sport and the sports establishment in society are able to suspend their critical faculties when it comes to support for their side or club.[4]

This is not the place to rehearse the many, now classic, examples of the pervasive role of politics and political motives in sporting practice throughout history. What is important to note here is the political potency of this myth, particularly in the Anglo-Saxon world where its popularity has been strongest. Politicians and others engaged in political activities, broadly defined, have had no hesitation in condemning those who would mix politics and sport, for their own political purposes and often to considerable popular effect. Both South African and New Zealand governments, in particular, on various occasions attacked domestic supporters of the sports boycott movement. Similarly, those who would attempt to promote the cause of change by interfering with normal sporting practice are keenly aware that their activities are liable to have particular force precisely because they can affect the consciousness of many citizens who would ordinarily have little interest in, or sympathy for, the causes they seek to promote. Although the targeting of sport by social critics may initially seem counter-productive, it can, over time, strongly reinforce processes of change. In the case of Springbok–All Black (South African–New Zealand) rugby links, for example, the myth of autonomy figured prominently. The fact that normal sports relations, passionately followed by thousands, became impossible in these two societies ultimately contributed substantially to processes of resocialisation, and thus to changing racial norms in both countries. Because of the cultural and political salience of rugby union in both societies, particularly in contests against each other, we examine the Springbok–All Black rugby relationship in close detail here and in chapter 5.

Sport as an instrument of political and economic elites

Thoroughly belying the myth of autonomy is the direct, self-conscious and instrumental use of sport by numerous governments of various ideological persuasions in the post-World War Two era and earlier. Governments have long supported physical education and sport as a means of fostering a healthy and economically productive work force in peace time, and a militarily effective populace in times of war. Sport has been seen as beneficial not only as a means of promoting fitness, but also for purposes of inculcating valued qualities of leadership and teamwork and as a means of social control, among other social purposes.[5] This has been true in such diverse contexts as the former Communist countries of the Eastern Bloc and the English public school tradition of the nineteenth century.

In an even more direct and overt fashion, some governments have sought to gain specific political advantages, both internationally and domestically, through the use of sport. Taylor emphasises three broad ways in which states have attempted to do this in the international sphere. First, a few states have given sport a central role in their foreign policies, 'presumably because they perceive the correct and successful practice of international sport will support their interests'.[6] Particularly noteworthy in this regard were several of the former Eastern Bloc countries, including East Germany and Cuba.[7] Second, all states have periodically found it useful to use sporting contacts to send both positive and negative diplomatic signals. And third, states have occasionally judged that in unusual circumstances private sporting contact might subvert its overall foreign policy and have therefore acted to forestall it. Several Olympic boycotts – including both the African boycott of the 1976 Olympics in protest over New Zealand's continuing rugby links with South Africa, and the boycott of the 1980 Moscow Olympics following the Soviet invasion of Afghanistan – have been based on this calculation.[8] Within these general parameters, a number of more specific international political roles may be identified – perhaps none more important than the pursuit of international prestige. This is particularly apparent in bids for major international sporting events, as well as in support for high performance sport holding out the promise of major international victories.[9] Certainly, the post-1994 African National Congress (ANC) led government of South Africa has placed great emphasis on the successes of the Rugby World Cup (RWC) of 1995 and the 1996 African Nations Cup of football (soccer) and provided strong support for the unsuccessful Cape Town 2004 Olympic bid.[10]

A rigid separation between domestic and international political spheres and motives is often inappropriate. Thus, many political purposes of sport have both international and domestic faces which are pursued simultaneously, in the manner of a 'two-level game'.[11] Here again, bids to host major sporting events and state support for high performance athletes are obvious examples, pointing to the most common of all political uses of sport: deliberate efforts at nation building and the forging of a common national identity. This instrumental purpose has been deliberately pursued with varying degrees of thoroughness and premeditation by states as diverse as Canada, the Soviet Union and numerous states in post-colonial Africa.[12] Its widespread appeal and utility, however, lies in the fact that sport seems naturally to foster feelings of intense community identity, so that even when governments and politicians do not seek to use it directly for nation- and identity-building purposes, sport is still liable to have political implications in this regard. As has been widely noted, sport's nation-building impact can be not unlike that of war.[13] This is true, it should be noted, right down to its differential and differentiated implications for males and females. We will return to the central theme of sport in the construction of national identity below.

Sport can also be used very effectively by political elites for rhetorical and communications purposes. Because of the pervasiveness of sport, sport imagery and analogies can be used to good advantage both as a means of communicating a particular political message, and as a way for politicians to project a folksy image, or the common touch. This has been amply displayed in the settler societies of the southern hemisphere – South Africa , New Zealand, Australia and Argentina – each of which has valued a self-image as a great sporting nation. The use of sporting images in political communications may have been taken to its highest levels by American presidents Richard Nixon and the great communicator himself, Ronald Reagan.[14]

We should point out that, in part because of the persistence of the myth of autonomy among the wider electorate in many societies, the instrumental use of sport by governing elites may have only a limited and ephemeral impact, and can indeed backfire. It is quite possible, in other words, that too strong and overt an intrusion into the treasured sphere of sport by politicians may be deeply resented by the bulk of sports fans, with negative ramifications for the perpetrator. Monnington has argued, for example, that the efforts of Margaret Thatcher – not a noted sports enthusiast – to intervene directly in the world of sports were ham-fisted and politically counter-productive.[15] Similarly, the use of sport in the Canadian referendum campaign on constitutional reform in 1992 by the political elites aligned behind the 'Charlottetown Accord' was arguably resented by the millions of fans whose passions had been aroused by the Toronto Blue Jays' run for baseball's World Series. Consequently, the use of baseball images in the pro-Accord advertising campaign was almost certainly ineffective, and quite possibly counter-productive.

Arguably considerably more safe and effective than the manipulation of sport by political elites has been its use by corporate elites for purposes of generating wealth and prestige. Indeed, it has been argued that perhaps *the* dominant trend in the organisation and practice of sport since the mid-1980s has been the advance of the 'commercial-professional ethos', and the concomitant 'rout' of the old 'amateur-elite ethos'.[16] This, of course, has profound political ramifications. Corporate interests have become extremely influential in the international and domestic politics of sport, along with sport governing bodies and various levels of government. Nowhere is this more apparent than in the Olympic movement, and in the organisation of major Olympic bids.

The role of leading corporate and economic interests in the politics surrounding rugby union is particularly intriguing. In its value structure, rugby has of course been one of the last bastions of the 'amateur-elite ethos' – a public face that has only recently fractured.[17] This has been a matter of some consequence in the particular political identities with which the sport has been associated and which it has reinforced in South Africa, New Zealand and elsewhere. This does not mean, however, that there has not been an important interrelationship between national economic elites and the rugby establishment in these countries, nor that there have not been important commercial influences upon it. Thus, the political interests and motives of leading economic interests *vis-à-vis* rugby in South Africa (especially when linked with New Zealand) is one of the areas on which we wish to shed new light.

Sport as a source of national identity

The most widely discussed and pervasive political role of sport is in the forging and reinforcing of community/national identities. John Hoberman has termed this near-universal characteristic 'sportive nationalism', and points out that it appears to have easily outlived the most extreme manifestations of political manipulation of sport under Eastern Bloc regimes. Clearly, the politicisation of sport in this respect is a much more widespread and deeply rooted phenomenon. As we have noted, sport's potential value for identity-building is something of which many political and social leaders have been keenly aware, and which they have attempted to manipulate for their own purposes. However, to reduce sport to a tool of political-economic elites – a superstructural 'opiate' effectively fostering false consciousness – as some neo-Marxist analysts were tempted to do in the 1970s and early 1980s, is both too crude and often inaccurate.[18] It undervalues the extent to which shared experiences and identities are fostered around sport quite independently of overt political manipulation. It also ignores the potentially progressive and oppositional activities which can be organised around sport, limited though they may be in the longer term. A more subtle understanding of sport's role in identity-building conceives of it as a central aspect of popular culture, which is in turn part of a broader, interdependent relationship or complex with the spheres of politics and production in any given society – an approach strongly influenced by Gramscian analysis.[19] Sport is an important locus of socialisation, political and otherwise, which can be deliberately fostered and manipulated, but which also has a dynamic and a life of its own.[20] As Hoberman notes in defining sportive nationalism, it is the 'ambition to see a nation's athletes excel in the inter-

6

national arena, [which can be] *promoted by a political elite or felt by many citizens without the promptings of national leaders'.*[21]

The specific content of the national identities fostered and reinforced by dominant sporting practices and rivalries is an area of particular fascination. Any sports enthusiast is liable to wax eloquent on the particular national styles of the strongest national sides in major international sports, and to expand on how these styles reflect their dominant cultural characteristics. Similarly, the origins of national sports and the sources of their special popularity in a given society will often be linked to distinct national cultural characteristics. Furthermore, particularly intense national rivalries (for example, Canada and Russia in hockey matches, Brazil and Argentina or England and Germany in soccer, and South Africa and New Zealand in rugby union) are often associated with much deeper social meanings, and are the occasion for extraordinary heights of collective emotion. While such discourses will frequently lapse into hyperbole and stereotype, they are not wholly without foundation. They can be a source of both admiration and resentment among the citizens/supporters of rival sides, and a source of national pride and/or angst, concerning traditional weaknesses or a national Achilles heel for example, among supporters of the home side.[22]

No less of a political analyst-practitioner than Henry Kissinger wrote engagingly about the national styles of major soccer powers in anticipation of the 1986 World Cup. According to Kissinger:

The German national team plays soccer the way its general staff prepared for war: its games are meticulously planned; each player is skilled in both attack and defence. . . . [However] the German national team suffers from the same disability as the famous Schlieffen plan on which German strategy in World War I was based . . . If the German team falls behind, or if its intricate approach yields no results, its game is shadowed by the underlying national premonition that in the end even the most dedicated effort will go unrewarded by the nightmare that ultimately fate is cruel.

On the other hand:

Brazilian teams display contagious exuberance; Brazilian fans cheer to the ecstatic beat of samba bands. Brazil always has the most acrobatic players; the individuals one cannot forget whatever the outcome of the match. But, as in Brazil's political institutions, this individualism is combined with an extraordinary ability to make the practical arrangements required for effective national performance [a questionable generalisation] . . . [However,] I have never seen an outstanding Brazilian goalkeeper . . . perhaps the only purely defensive assignment on a team offends the Brazilian self-image.[23]

Do these sport-linked identities matter in any substantial socio-political sense? Are they more than a source of recreation and escapism? Grant Jarvie rightly notes that 'there is a great danger in overemphasising the role of sport in the making of nations'.[24] Certainly, one must guard against reading too much into the heated talk of sports fans. Nevertheless, a more searching and critical investigation of the particular meanings of various sport-based identities suggests that they play a multi-faceted and diffuse role in cultural development and socialisation, with significant political consequences.

For one thing, it has been speculated that international sport plays a role of heightened symbolic significance 'for smaller nations that have few opportunities to assert themselves against much larger states'.[25] This generalisation cannot be pushed too far: one need only think of the role of sport in the United States, the former Soviet Union or contemporary China to recognise that sport can be a matter of high-level political concern in even the largest and most powerful of countries. Nevertheless, there is much evidence to support the view that sport and sporting triumphs are matters of particular significance for relatively small or otherwise weak societies in international terms. They are seen to underscore the world class qualities, the special genius, of societies that cannot hope to triumph with regularity in the arenas of international military or economic power. This proposition is particularly pertinent when considering the political salience of rugby in South Africa. Traditionally, white South Africans have taken exceptional pride in, and placed extraordinary emphasis upon, their global mastery of this sport and of other nations who play rugby. Its political symbolism for them has been, therefore, much more than a matter of simple recreation. Only in New Zealand has rugby consistently played a similarly dynamic role over the twentieth century.[26] Concomitantly, their widely recognised mastery of, and passion for, rugby raised the international political significance of the Springbok–All Black rivalry to a matter of high-level political concern and, in a few places, intense political struggle in the context of the broader struggle against apartheid. In a very real sense, therefore, sport can matter for small societies collectively in a manner which is far from trivial. This is readily apparent in the seriousness with which both political leaders and critical social movements in New Zealand and South Africa treated the issue of rugby links, as we shall see. In line with Stoddart's analysis of the role of Caribbean cricket, it is fruitful in such contexts 'to approach sport as a constant and complex political factor inextricably bound up with the cultural evolution of the society within which it is located'.[27]

Beyond this significance in relation to the creation of a common national identity, however, it is important to recognise the role of sport in defining and differentiating identities *within* these national societies. For example, in all societies, sport has contributed significantly to gender socialisation and differentiation. In the major team sports that are the focus of mass popularity in most societies, males are the athletes, the coaches, the administrators – the celebrated heroes embodying the hopes and loyalties of the nation. Women are the keepers of the home front, the long-suffering and loyal supporters who foster a comfortable and comforting environment to ensure that the athlete is able to achieve his full performance potential. Thus, the national identity with which sport is bound up has very different implications for men and women, and is very much male-centred. The role of rugby in defining and reinforcing gender relations in South Africa is therefore a matter of considerable interest and political consequence, especially given the rugby club's traditional status as an exclusive 'male preserve'.[28]

Similarly, sport plays a powerful role in relation to sexual orientation and the definition of 'normality' in virtually all societies. As in most military establishments, major team sports have resolutely and rigidly defined homosexuality as deviant, exerting in turn a powerful influence on the norms of the wider societies within which they are embedded. Yet the relationship between sexual orientation and sport is a complex one in socio-psychological terms: particularly in contact sports like rugby, there is a very high degree of same-sex physical intimacy. Again, the treatment of sexual orientation in male and female sport differs significantly, with a much higher level of tolerance of homosexuality in female sports, but with a clear if tacit understanding concerning public silence.[29]

One could go on at considerable length concerning the differential role of sport in defining and reinforcing various social cleavages. Often, for example, sport is closely tied up with class, community and generational identities. Of particular interest in an analysis of rugby in South Africa, however, is its role in the making and remaking of identities in an ethnically and racially plural society. By way of comparison, in New Zealand, another ethnically diverse country which has nurtured a somewhat misleading identity as a tolerant multi-racial society, sport in general, and rugby above all, has served to reinforce this identity. Maoris have almost always been skilled and celebrated members of All Black sides; and in the early days of agitation against rugby links with South Africa, the issue was not so much about racial policies and conditions in South Africa, as the widespread insistence that New Zealand representative sides should include both white and Maori members selected on the basis of merit. The rallying cry 'No Maoris, No Tour' came rather late in the history of Springbok–All Black rugby, with the New Zealand rugby establishment – closely related in turn to the country's political and economic establishment – long tolerating the exclusion of Maoris from South African tours in deference to South African racial sensibilities.[30] Thus, New Zealand multi-racialism has historically been a weak and partial phenomenon.

In South Africa, on the other hand, sport traditionally played a prominent role in reinforcing rigidly distinct racial, or racially based community identities. Rugby, in particular, became intimately tied up with Afrikanerdom: 'rugby had a *symbolic* significance which predisposed Afrikaners not merely to play it but to *identify* with the game, in such measure that to some extent they have transformed it in their own image'.[31] Defining precisely what it is about the characteristics of rugby which led to this powerful association is a fascinating exercise. Several authors have contrasted its profoundly collectivist ethos with the 'individualism and showmanship' characteristic of soccer, and have linked its communal yet autocratic tendencies to the character of traditional Afrikaner culture and nationalism. According to Archer and Bouillon, '*Personal self- denial* in the service of the group, *collective discipline* in the prosecution of a general cause, all explicit components of Afrikanerdom, were among the implicit virtues of rugby – a game which the Springboks have conquered above all by their ferocious collective discipline'.[32] More recently, Desiree Lewis has argued that 'Generally, the playing of rugby is an enactment of hegemony, a display of *kragdadigheid*'.[33] On the other hand, soccer has been associated with the culture of the black townships: 'deft and spectacular, it forms part of an ethos of frenetic enthusiasm amidst socio-economic deprivation'.[34]

The situation is not so clear-cut in practice, however. Each of the major team sports in South Africa enjoys considerable popularity beyond its ethnic/racial core constituency. Rugby specifically helps to define the ambiguous and vulnerable cultural identity of the mixed-race or 'Coloured' population.[35] Among this group, rugby holds a place of prominence comparable to that which it holds among Afrikaners, illustrating the important fact that in many respects South Africa's coloureds share as much in common with Afrikaner culture as with urban African culture. In the Eastern Cape, however, rugby has also played an important part within urban African popular culture as it spread outwards from mission schools. Key figures within the ANC elite, such as Nelson

Mandela and Steve Tshwete, played rugby when they were younger. Thus, rugby has been significant beyond the confines of white South African popular culture, notwithstanding the widely held conviction among most white South Africans to the contrary. We examine the role of rugby in Coloured and, to a lesser degree, African communities in chapter 3 below.

In the face of international isolation, all major sports organisations in South Africa developed various affirmative action or outreach pro-grammes during the 1980s – with rugby's being, not surprisingly, the most controversial. These programmes were widely denigrated by anti-apartheid forces as transparent tokenism, often quite properly. Nevertheless, they arguably played a significant role in the vital task of attempting to resocialise South African whites, in particular, and in breaking down the norms of racial exclusivity and separation that were a major obstacle to fundamental social change in South Africa as a whole. What remains to be seen is the role sport-based socialisation and identi-ties may play in either fostering or inhibiting the difficult trek from apartheid to fundamental (structural) social reform, and the specific place and role of rugby in the emergent dispensation. We will come to this issue at the end of this book.

Thus, while it is wise to reiterate a note of caution about reading too much into the role of sport in constructing identities and socialising groups and individuals, that it plays *some* role in this regard cannot be denied. Indeed, that it can play a *prominent and important* role, with sig-nificant political consequences, is a proposition which bears serious investigation. How, then, has the role of sport been theorised in socio-political analysis? And can we generalise about the overall weight of its influence – whether conservative or oppositional – in politics and society?

Theorising the role of sport in socio-political analysis

Although serious social scientific analysis of sport is relatively new, it has by now stimulated a growing and increasingly sophisticated body of theoretical literature. The objective of this section is not to offer a com-prehensive review of this literature or to revisit old debates, but rather to highlight several dominant alternative approaches and tendencies, in order to frame the discussion of subsequent chapters. It will be sug-gested that while sport has generally played a conservative role in society, celebrating and reinforcing the status quo, there is nothing

11

inevitable about this role. Indeed, sport can be an important focus for oppositional organisation and reformist social movements.

To summarise, one can identify three broad tendencies in the debate on the role of sport in politics and society. Each of these tendencies subsumes a variety of interpretations and approaches, some of which may be quite distinct and competitive. Nevertheless, it is useful for our purposes to group the literature into functionalist approaches, which view sport as a constructive and integrative influence in society; critical and structuralist materialist approaches – or 'conflict theories'[36] – which view it as a vehicle manipulated by dominant class forces to reinforce socio-economic hierarchy and inequality; and various 'idealist' approaches, which view culture, and sport within it, as an important and real socio-political influence, whether in conjunction with material and political forces or more autonomously.[37]

The earliest efforts to theorise the role of sport in society, emerging from the discipline of sociology, came out of the functionalist tradition. Jay Coakley has labelled this tendency 'sport as an inspiration'.[38] From this perspective, sport is seen as 'an adaptive response on the part of society and/or the part of specific groups within society, to change, which is worked out in the cultural realm'.[39] In other words, it facilitates system maintenance and adaptation – and is therefore functional to the system as a whole – by helping it to meet four fundamental needs: the need for pattern maintenance and tension management; the need for integration; the need for goal attainment; and the need for adaptation.[40] As Coakley and others have noted, this approach shares much with the common sense or conventional wisdom of sport as a positive and constructive influence in society, inculcating important values and disciplines, serving as a source of role models for youth, and so on. It presupposes a benign or indeed celebratory view of the society in question – as a structure which *should* be preserved and adapted, rather than changed. It has been rightly criticised for this uncritical and undifferentiated view of society, and of sport's role therein. Yet it is also useful in highlighting the integrative potential of sport: its capacity to generate powerful and passionately felt shared loyalties and experiences.

The second broad tendency in the literature has been termed by Coakley 'conflict theory', or 'sport as an opiate'. In contrast with functionalist approaches, this approach begins from a sharply critical analysis of capitalist society and of the social divisions and inequalities it is seen to generate. It locates its theoretical roots in various neo-Marxist approaches, including the Frankfurt School of critical social theory, which interprets sport as 'an integral part of a system of class domination and exploitation', and structuralist approaches, which see it as one among several 'ideological state apparatuses' vital in the reproduction of class relations.[41] From these types of perspectives, sport is seen to perform a variety of functions, all fundamentally serving the interests of those in positions of dominance: for example, alienating people from their own bodies; maintaining social control; facilitating capital accumulation through its commercialisation and commodification; and fostering false and dangerous ideologies of nationalism, militarism and sexism.

This theoretical tendency clearly exposes some persistent historical characteristics in the use and abuse of sport – some of the ways in which elites have attempted to manipulate it for their own purposes. It provides a useful corrective to the uncritical and benign view of society taken by functionalist approaches. Yet in its relentlessly negative view of the socio-political implications of organised sport, and in its general tendency to see everywhere the manipulative and controlling influence of dominant classes, it falls into a comparable trap of over-generalisation and over-simplification. It can similarly be accused of failing to recognise the diversity and complexity of the influence of sport in various societies. Coakley neatly captures these parallel weaknesses in addressing the question: is sport an inspiration or an opiate? He argues that 'the way people answer this question depends on what they think about the society in which sport exists'.[42]

More recently, there has been something of a convergence between more radical and orthodox approaches to the study of sport, emphasising the reality and importance of people's cultural experiences and values as political forces in their own right, and sport's potential to have both a constructive and destructive influence in society. This tendency is loosely labelled 'idealist' here, not because it asserts the unchallenged primacy of values and ideas (in most cases, at least), but rather because it asserts the substance and significance of their role *alongside* material and political structures and forces. This is notably true of approaches coming from the more radical side of the spectrum, inspired primarily by the work of Antonio Gramsci. Gramscian analysis stresses the central concept of hegemony and hegemonic orders in society, based on a harmonisation of dominant cultural/ideological, material and political forces. These specifically historical orders and forms of class domination are maintained with relatively limited resort to coercion by persuading most members of the society that they constitute the natural or normal order of things. Such approaches therefore give substantial weight to cultural practices, notably including sport, in explaining the nature and persistence of political-economic orders. They also lead to an emphasis on oppositional organisation and activity around sport as a meaningful aspect of broader counter-hegemonic struggles.[43] Concurrently, a few theorists have extended Gramscian concepts to the analysis of the international system, positing the outlines of an emergent transnational hegemony and also 'transnational counter-hegemonic forces', of which the international anti-apartheid movement and the sports boycott movement more specifically may be seen as examples.[44] These types of approaches seem to promise a more fruitful and sophisticated analysis of the relationship between sport and politics, giving sport real weight without exaggerating its autonomy and influence. They inform the discussion that follows.

Can we then generalise about the overall weight of sport's influence in politics and society? On balance, it is probably fair to conclude that it has most often been a conservative, status quo oriented influence in society. For example, it has tended to reinforce patriarchal attitudes, it has been widely supported by social and political elites in an effort to maintain social control, and it has been used to encourage values supportive of the status quo – most notably patriotism. Coakley points out that 'it is probably true that athletes and fans are more likely than other people to have attitudes supportive of the status quo',[45] although he also notes that the degree to which sport is influential in actually *shaping* these attitudes is somewhat less certain.

Yet to argue that sport has generally exercised a conservative influence in most societies and polities should not obscure its liberating and reformist potential. This potential can be exercised at a variety of levels. It can be exercised at the level of the individual athlete, for whom sport 'can be a personally creative, expressive, and liberating experience'.[46] It is also possible that individual athletes or groups of athletes can use the popular platform which sporting success provides to challenge the status quo or social injustices, often with significant popular impact.[47] In certain instances, furthermore, sport-induced patriotism can be an oppositional and liberating force, at least to some degree – as in the nationalist struggles of the Irish. In South Africa, Desiree Williams argues, the 'psycho-existential resistance' afforded by black soccer has at times been 'yoked to an overt political agenda', as in the integration of soccer matches in the townships during the 1970s and 1980s with Black Consciousness Movement (BCM) and United Demcratic Front (UDF) rallies.[48] Many

Coloured and African rugby fans in Cape Town and Port Elizabeth openly cheered for visiting international teams when they played the Springboks between the 1930s and 1990s, venting their frustration at South African racial exclusivist practices while also celebrating their love of rugby. In some instances, furthermore, the disruption of normal sporting practice, closely associated with the status quo, can be an important component of wider social struggles – as in the national and transnational sport boycott movements of the 1970s and 1980s. Finally, in other historical contexts, social reconciliation and integration must be viewed as desirable and indeed necessary; and insofar as sport can be useful in encouraging these tendencies, its influence must be regarded as socially and politically progressive. As Jarvie summarises, 'sporting traditions themselves, whether they are invented or not, can be both integrative and divisive, conservative and oppositional'.[49] In the case of South African rugby, and the political activities which have surrounded it, both the conservative and oppositional potential of sport is readily apparent.

Sport in world politics

To summarise, sport can be a diverse and complex source of influence in politics both within and between national societies and states. Its political significance is rooted in its central roles in popular culture and socialisation. It can and has been used in a self-conscious and instrumental fashion by political and economic elites in various social contexts; it has also, less routinely, been exploited instrumentally by counter-hegemonic social movements, as in the sports boycott movement, or in grass-roots coalitions opposing high profile Olympic bids. But beyond its instrumental uses, sport can have a less direct and more pervasive influence through its socialising impact – in fostering socio-cultural cohesion and dominant social values or, alternatively, in serving as a focus for social disruption and change.

Traditionally, political analysis has been divided into sharply differentiated national and international spheres. There was politics *within* national states, in the context of which national governments might wish to use sports policies for certain purposes; and there was politics *between* states, in which various 'instruments of statecraft' – diplomacy, military force, economic sanctions – were brought to bear. Sport could be used in this arena as an adjunct to these instruments of statecraft: as a means of signalling diplomatic disapproval or as a preliminary step in seeking diplomatic rapprochement, for example.

Although these separate spheres still have some analytical utility, the picture has become considerably muddier since the 1970s. Increasingly, corporations, social movements and international organisations exercise political influence both within and *across* national boundaries. Moreover, modern communications technologies – above all television – have the potential to make cultural practices and crises in particular societies into global concerns. Shared cultural practices can lead to the assumption of a tangible interest and indeed right to intervene in the affairs of foreign states, both by governments and, more typically, by non-governmental organisations. We live in an era, in sum, in which the old model of international relations needs to be replaced by a more complex model of world politics, embodying inter-, trans- and sub-national actors, exercising influence within, across and between national societies.

There is nothing terribly new about these observations. Nevertheless, because they fly in the face of so much conventional wisdom, they bear reassertion. It is our argument that the politics surrounding rugby in South Africa and especially rugby between the South African national Springbok team and other rugby-playing nations provides a particularly clear illustration of both the internal role of sport and sporting culture in politics and the transnationalisation of world politics. It illustrates, for example, the degree to which internal social and cultural issues can become intense political concerns in far-distant societies, the degree to which effective political co-operation and alliances can be forged across national boundaries by groups operating at cross-purposes with their respective national governments, and so on. It is a rich and complex story, which belies simple conceptions of the sources of power, influence and change in world politics. It is a story which deserves to be more widely exposed and studied.

As we analyse the ways that rugby, politics and culture are intertwined in South Africa, we begin with an examination of the imperial origins and connections that surrounded the game in the late nineteenth and early twentieth centuries. It is important to understand these imperial connections of rugby as they remain strong into the post-apartheid era. Rugby emerged out of a whole range of British sports that were exported throughout the British Empire in the late nineteenth century. Sports such as rugby and cricket were promoted as cultural links between 'home' in Britain and British settlers and officials overseas. As these sports expanded into the training of colonial indigenous elites, British team games became linked to measures of 'civilisation'. This was certainly the case in South Africa as rugby and cricket were taught by missionaries and in elite black schools. Chapter 3 therefore examines the development of Coloured and African rugby in the twentieth century as both part of the imperial project and as rugby in black communities developed its own cultural dynamics. Chapter 4 then turns to a central issue for the understanding of rugby, politics and power relations in South Africa, that is, the ways that the Afrikaner nationalist movement in general and the government and its supporting nationalist structures in particular co-opted rugby as part of their nationalist project, and were in turn moved to contemplate modifications to that project to protect international rugby links. In this context, international rugby played by the Springbok national team became the pinnacle of the nation at play, generating high levels of passion and intensity amongst fans and serving to strengthen national (white and Afrikaner) identification. Most especially, international matches against the New Zealand All Blacks and the British Lions, when they toured South Africa, were invested with special meaning. For Afrikaners, beating *die Englse* represented in the Lions was certainly significant; however, matches against the All Blacks were for world supremacy. Indeed, New Zealanders were the one other country that seemed to take rugby as seriously as many white South Africans thought it should be taken. As a result, protests against Springbok–All Black rugby struck at the heart of white South African society and identity. In Chapter 5 we turn to the specific links between South Africa and New Zealand as the two dominant rugby powers of the twentieth century. We are particularly concerned with how both states supported the rugby relationship and how transnational organisations campaigned to stop contests between the two nations. In many respects, it was the continuing rugby contact between South Africa and New Zealand that was the most crucial point of sanctions pressure in sports and the one given the most attention by political authorities hoping to manage any changes to apartheid on their own terms. This case study demonstrates just how significant South African–New Zealand rugby was in the entire sports boycott debate, a point underestimated by virtually all Western observers writing from outside of New Zealand. Significantly, South Africa's return to official international rugby in 1992 was made against the All Blacks.

The final three chapters turn to the role of rugby in the transition from apartheid to post-apartheid South Africa. We first examine the process of change itself, one which involved the South African Rugby Board (SARB) and establishment provincial associations, Coloured and African associations affiliated to SARB and non-racial organisations, principally the South African Rugby Union (SARU), affiliated to the oppositional South African Council of Sport (SACOS). The process of unity in rugby occurred ahead of and during the transition from the apartheid to the post-apartheid eras and was accomplished by early 1992. In that year South Africa returned to international rugby (as well as to the Olympic Games – it had already returned to international cricket), playing tests against the All Blacks and the reigning World Cup champions, the Australian Wallabies. While cricket and other sporting organisations that became unified appeared to be beacons of national unity, rugby lagged behind. At the first test against New Zealand held at Ellis Park, old South African flags were waved fervently by the white-dominated crowd in apparent defiance of the wider changes taking place outside the rugby ground. Ironically, in 1995, rugby emerged as the most significant unifying force, albeit momentarily, in the new South Africa. In chapter 7 we discuss at length the 1995 RWC hosted and won by South Africa as it offered a moment of national reconciliation and unity. The moment of unity was to be short-lived, however, as white rugby officials refused to embrace the reconciliatory potential unleashed by the RWC. Additionally, the sport went professional causing internal tensions between players and administrators. During 1996 a string of successive defeats merged with rising discontent to return rugby towards the days of 1992 rather than the euphoria of 1995. Finally, in late 1996 and 1997 crises within rugby circles including racism and alleged maladministration continued and culminated in the launching of an official inquiry into the running of rugby. In the final chapter we turn to some of the events in the aftermath of the World Cup and the problems that have beset rugby ever since as it remains dominated by a power elite that controlled in the game during the apartheid era.

Notes

1 For a recent example of work on sport and politics in various national contexts, see V. Duke and L. Crolley, *Football, Nationality and the State* (London, Longman, 1996).

2 L. Allison, 'The changing context of sporting life', in L. Allison (ed.), *The Changing Politics of Sport* (Manchester, Manchester University Press, 1993), p. 5; E. Morse, 'Sport and Canadian foreign policy', *Behind the Headlines*, 45:2 (1987), p. 2.

3 Allison, 'The changing context of sporting life', pp. 5–6.

4 Many who provide radical critiques of sport are labelled 'anti-sport' by those who profess to love sport. This has led to a number of cross-accusations between historians and sociologists of sport, for example.

5 For a discussion of this process in several contexts, see the essays in J. Nauright and T. J. L. Chandler (eds), *Making Men: Rugby and Masculine Identity* (London, Frank Cass, 1996).
6 T. Taylor, 'Sport and world politics: functionalism and the state system', *International Journal*, 43:4 (1988), p. 550.
7 T. Slack and D. Whitson, 'The place of sport in Cuba's foreign relations', *International Journal*, 43:4 (1988). For East Germany, see T. Magdalinski, 'Reconstructing Identities: *Traditionspflege*, History, Sport and National Identity in the German Democratic Republic, 1970–79', unpublished PhD thesis, The University of Queensland, Australia, 1996.
8 Taylor, 'Sport and world politics', pp. 550–1.
9 For example, see Morse, 'Sport and Canadian foreign policy', p. 5.
10 We discuss the RWC below. For a detailed discussion of the role of sport in the new South Africa, see J. Nauright, *Sport, Cultures and Identities in South Africa* (London, Leicester University Press, 1997 and Cape Town, David Phillip, 1997). For a good discussion of South Africa and the national rugby team during the RWC, see D. Booth, 'Mandela and *Amabokoboko*: the political and linguistic nationalisation of South Africa?', *The Journal of Modern African Studies*, 34:3 (1996), pp. 459–77; and Albert Grundlingh, 'From redemption to recidivism? Rugby and change in South Africa during the 1995 Rugby World Cup and its aftermath', paper presented to the Sporting Traditions XI conference of the Australian Society for Sports History, Perth, July 1997.
11 On two-level games, see R. Putnam, 'Diplomacy and domestic politics: the logic of two-level games', *International Organization*, 42 (1988), pp. 427–60.
12 For examples, see G. Caldwell, 'International sport and national identity', *International Social Science Journal*, 34:2 (1982); J. Hoberman, 'Sport and ideology in the post-Communist age', in Allison (ed.), *The Changing Politics of Sport*, p. 19; and R. Uwechue, 'Nation building and sport in Africa', in B. Lowe, D. Kanin and A. Strenk (eds), *Sport and International Relations* (Champaign, Stipes Publishing Co., 1978).
13 For examples, see J. Phillips, 'Rugby, war, and the mythology of the New Zealand Male', *New Zealand Journal of History*, 18:2 (1984); M. Phillips, 'Football, class and war: the rugby codes in New South Wales, 1907–1918', in Nauright and Chandler (eds), *Making Men*.
14 T. Monnington, 'Politicians and sport: uses and abuses', in Allison (ed.), *The Changing Politics of Sport*, pp. 125–9.
15 Monnington, 'Politicians and sport', pp. 141–9.
16 Allison, 'The changing context of sporting life', pp. 6–10; Hoberman, 'Sport and ideology', pp. 16–18.
17 The Gaelic Athletic Association, perhaps ironically, is the last major Western team sports organisation that remains amateur. For comment on rugby union, see Allison, 'The changing context of sporting life', pp. 8–9; S. Jones, *Endless Winter: The Inside Story of the Rugby Revolution* (Edinburgh, Mainstream Publishing, 1994).
18 For an example, see John Hargreaves, 'Sport, culture and ideology', in Jennifer Hargreaves (ed.), *Sport, Culture and Ideology* (London, Routledge and Kegan Paul, 1982), pp. 41–6.
19 Hargreaves, 'Sport, culture and ideology', pp. 47–50; Allison, 'The changing context of sporting life', pp. 4–5.
20 The best discussion of sport, resistance and power relationships from a

Gramscian perspective to date is S. G. Jones, *Sport, Politics and the Working Class: Organised Labour and Sport in Interwar Britain* (Manchester, Manchester University Press, 1988).

21 Hoberman, 'Sport and ideology', p. 16. Emphasis added.

22 Joe Maguire discusses the angst issues in analysing media accounts of British sporting disasters and the problems of John Major, see J. Maguire, 'Sport, identity politics, and globalization', *Sociology of Sport Journal*, 11:4 (1994), pp. 398–427; for an account of some similar processes in Canada, see J. Nauright and P. White, 'Nostalgia, community, and nation: professional hockey and football in Canada', *AVANTE*, 2:3 (1996), pp. 24–41.

23 H. Kissinger, 'How soccer reflects national attitudes', *The Australian*, 30 June 1986.

24 G. Jarvie, 'Sport, nationalism and cultural identity', in Allison (ed.), *The Changing Politics of Sport*, p. 78.

25 Hoberman, 'Sport and ideology', p. 21; also see B. Stoddart, 'Caribbean cricket: the role of sport in emerging small-nation politics', *International Journal*, 43:4 (1988), pp. 618–42.

26 Some would argue that rugby has also played a similar role in Wales, though the dynamics of rugby and nation in South Africa and New Zealand work a little differently, not least because the latter are politically sovereign states.

27 Stoddart, 'Caribbean cricket', p. 619.

28 K. Sheard and E. Dunning, 'The rugby football club as a type of "male preserve": some sociological notes', in J. Loy, G. Kenyon and B. McPherson (eds), *Sport, Culture and Society*, 2nd edition (Philadelphia, Lea and Febiger, 1981); S. Thompson, 'Challenging the hegemony: New Zealand's women's opposition to rugby and the reproduction of a capitalist patriarchy', *International Review for the Sociology of Sport*, 23:3 (1988); C. Dann, 'The game is over', *Broadsheet* (New Zealand), 97 (1982).

29 K. Bohls and M. Wangrin, 'Athletes revel in being one of the guys, not one of the gays', *Globe and Mail* (Toronto), 4 August 1993.

30 For a detailed discussion of this, see J. Nauright, '"Like fleas on a dog": emerging national and international conflict over New Zealand rugby ties with South Africa,' *Sporting Traditions*, 10:1 (1993), pp. 54–77.

31 R. Archer and A. Bouillon, *The South African Game: Sport and Racism* (London, Zed Press, 1982), p.65.

32 Archer and Bouillon, *The South African Game*, p. 72.

33 D. Lewis, 'Soccer and rugby: popular productions of pleasure in South African culture', *Southern African Political and Economic Monthly*, 6:3–4 (1992/93), p. 15. *Kragdadigheid* in this context refers to rugby as a display of efficient vigour and energy.

34 Lewis, 'Soccer and rugby', p. 13.

35 It is well known that the labelling of different 'population groups' in South Africa was, and remains, deeply politicised. Our practice in this book conforms to current norms – that is, 'black' South Africans will be used to refer to all 'non-white' population groups collectively, including 'coloured', Indian and African South Africans.

36 J. Coakley, 'Sport in society: an inspiration or an opiate?', in D. S. Eitzen (ed.), *Sport in Contemporary Society* (New York, St. Martin's Press, 1989), pp. 29–37.

37 For sophisticated and more extensive treatments of these alternative tenden-

cies, see the essays by Jennifer and John Hargreaves in Jennifer Hargreaves (ed.), *Sport, Culture and Ideology*.
38 Coakley, 'Sport in society: an inspiration or an opiate?'.
39 John Hargreaves, 'Sport, culture and ideology', p. 35.
40 Coakley, 'Sport in society: an inspiration or an opiate', pp. 24–30.
41 Coakley, 'Sport in society: an inspiration or an opiate?', pp. 30–7; John Hargreaves, 'Sport, culture and ideology', pp. 41–7.
42 Coakley, 'Sport in society: an inspiration or an opiate?', p. 37.
43 For example, see G. Jarvie, *Class, Race and Sport in South Africa's Political Economy* (London, Routledge and Kegan Paul, 1985).
44 R. Cox, *Power, Production and the World Order* (New York, Columbia University Press, 1987).
45 Coakley, 'Sport in society: an inspiration or an opiate?', p. 36.
46 Coakley, 'Sport in society: an inspiration or an opiate?', p. 36.
47 Examples might include: the handful of rugby All Blacks who declined invitations to play in test series against the Springboks; some high-profile sportsmen and sportswomen in South Africa who forsook the prestige and rewards of 'white' establishment sport to play in non-racial leagues; the black American athletes who gave the Black Power salute during medal presentation ceremonies at the Mexico Olympics; and the organisers of the Gay Games.
48 Lewis, 'Soccer and rugby', p. 16.
49 Jarvie, 'Sport, nationalism and cultural identity', p. 73.

Chapter 2

Making imperial men:
the emergence of white rugby
in South Africa

My immediate lessons were religious. The religion was called Sport. The holy altar was Rugby. God was the captain of the First XV. The angels were his team-mates. Any boy who bunked watching a home game for the Firsts was flogged and cast into darkness, a hissing and a byword and probably a homo. (Patrick Lee writing about being at Hilton College, Natal, in 1966.)[1]

While Africans migrated south into present day South Africa some 2000 years ago and the Dutch began to settle in and around Cape Town from 1652, it was only with the arrival of permanent British control supported by the weight of British imperial power in 1806 that economic, cultural and political power began to spread throughout the region. The British felt themselves to be superior in culture, economics and political structures when compared to other groups of people thus leading to a promotion of things British to other societies, while incorporating little of local cultures from the Empire into dominant British cultural practices. By the mid-nineteenth century a wide range of British cultural practices pervaded both the British Isles and the British Empire where the sun appeared never to set on afternoon teas, cricket and other sporting matches and the reading of Shakespeare. It was in this climate that British sports arrived in South Africa during the nineteenth century.

Significantly, white residents in southern Africa adopted many of the sports played by British elites, sports that also dominated white settler societies such as Australia and New Zealand. By the early 1900s regular rugby and cricket tours took place between South Africa and the British Isles establishing a pattern of close sporting relations linking South Africa with imperial power and a broader international order that valorised white dominance. The rise of white sports in South Africa occurred as racial attitudes hardened and the development of rugby demonstrates the racially divisive power of the segregated system as this chapter and the next discuss. While legislative politics remained outside of rugby, the development of the sport was conditioned by the wider policies of segregation and later apartheid, informed first by a British concept of cultural difference based on race and later on theories of racial separation promoted by Afrikaner intellectuals and the Afrikaner nationalist movement. In South Africa, sport in general and rugby in particular became central cultural elements in the emergence and maintenance of geographies of exclusion and division that conditioned the entrenchment of divergent sporting cultures among spatially divided groups.

This chapter concentrates on the development of white, imperially connected rugby and the next will focus on rugby in the black communities. Both white and black rugby, however, emerged from a strong imperial background and were situated in the wider process of sporting expansion emanating from Britain during the nineteenth century and thus must be discussed within the wider development of British sports in South Africa. It was to white rugby, along with a few other sports such as cricket, however, that ruling elites attached the greatest political and social significance. By the time of the formation of the Union of South Africa in 1910, politicians hosted public functions for leading local and visiting sports teams and players, thus linking the public face of the state within sporting successes and international sporting links. South Africa's close ties to imperial and Western international sporting structures were strong into the 1960s when moves to isolate South Africa because of apartheid began to affect sport. South Africa's return to international sport in the 1990s, however, has been warmly welcomed by many of its former competitors, most especially the white-dominated countries of the former British Empire with whom the old white South African sporting teams had close relations. In order to understand just why such reactions were so strong, we need to situate the development of South African sports within the broader imperial and global context, particularly within a white old-boy cultural order that pervaded imperial societies.

While the formative period in South African sports was crucial in laying the foundations for South Africa's position in modern sports, surprisingly little academic attention has been paid to the emergence of imperial sporting forms and culture. Robert Morrell has recently examined the links between imperial culture, masculinity and rugby union in Natal and Burridge Spies has discussed the imperial connection in rugby union in a small overview.[2] The most thorough source for early rugby history, however, remains Ivor Difford's history written in 1933.[3] Despite the relative lack of academic analysis, it is possible to examine the emergence of rugby union, its links with a broader imperial sporting culture and its early connection to politics as we attempt to situate international sanctions debates surrounding sport and the role of politics within South African sport in historical context. It will then be possible to see just how powerful the links between sport and politics have been on a whole range of levels when applied to the analysis of sport in South Africa and South African sport in the international arena.

British sport in South Africa and imperial connections

Many modern sports and sporting organisations emerged in Britain in the middle decades of the nineteenth century coinciding with Britain's undisputed dominance as a world power. The British navy controlled the seas and British shipping linked a global trading system. As a result, British sports soon spread to areas of British influence overseas with cricket, horse racing and varieties of football soon appearing in South America, Africa, India and Australasia. South Africa quickly developed British sporting forms after British settlers began arriving in the 1820s. By the 1870s, South African settlers were playing most British sports, many of which were only just becoming codified such as soccer (1863) and rugby union (1871) and soon became linked to a wider imperial sporting community. Before the building of the Suez Canal in the 1880s, Cape Town was on the main shipping routes to Asia and Australasia placing it in a central position to receive British cultural developments and contacts from those going back to Britain from India or Australia. English-speaking white schools in South Africa took up British games and used them to help instil values of British elite culture.[4] These games took on a greater significance in a colonial context where whites were a small minority of the population. Educationalists and elites repeatedly equated civilisation with Britishness and whiteness. Although the virtues of British civilisation and cultural behaviour were promoted on mission stations to a small percentage of the African population, British culture represented cultural, moral and even genetic or natural superiority to British settlers and officials that set them apart from the local population. Indeed, for many years British settlers all over the Empire referred to Britain as 'home' rather than the places they lived. Deference in all cultural matters, including sport, went to Britain and British institutions and authorities. By the early 1900s, however, sport was the one cultural activity where colonial men gained a measure of equality and even dominance as the British and colonial media frequently stated.[5]

Cricket and rugby union became the team sports that most closely drew white imperial societies together through sport and were sports to which colonial leaders gave official support. While rugby and other forms of football received attention as excellent games for young men as early as the 1850s, many elite British men originally thought cricket to be the game which best reflected manliness. By the early 1900s, however, earlier concepts of manliness were transformed into a muscular Christianity that focused more explicitly on physical activity as preparation for war rather than on moral superiority.[6] Social commentators by 1900 frequently asserted that the best determinants of the relative physical condition of two nations during peacetime were sporting contests. Arguments focused on the links between sport, nationalism and masculinity. The *Quarterly Review* asserted in 1904 that 'The national character is more deeply influenced by such popular pastimes as cricket, football . . . and the large class of amusements which may be generically termed ball games.'[7]

Of all sports, rugby by 1900 was viewed as the 'best trial of the relative vigour and virility of any two or more opposing countries'.[8] Thus, rugby began to replace cricket in the minds of many as the game most reflective of the manhood of a nation, although in most of England and Scotland rugby union remained the football code of the middle and upper classes. Losses at rugby, according to social observers of the day, reflected the relative state of the British power elite's manhood. Therefore, losses to colonials at rugby in 1905, 1906, 1908 and 1912 confirmed for many that the elite of the British race was deteriorating. Colonial teams were better trained, fitter and more innovative in their style of play, which contrasted sharply with the traditionalism prevalent among English club and county rugby sides. In particular, the spectacular successes of the 1905 New Zealand All Blacks and the 1906–7 and 1912 South African Springboks shocked those who might have been complacent about the state of middle- and upper-class masculine vitality. In addition, these colonial victories gave South African and New Zealand settlers a sense of achievement, of a collective national self-worth that came as movements towards Dominion, or nation, status gathered force.

In the late nineteenth and early twentieth centuries an Empire-wide public school educated class forged close links in which sport was a central element. Sporting contacts between Britain and the 'white' colonies became highly visible links of Empire from the 1860s, and especially from 1878 when the first official Australian cricket team toured England. On 27 May 1878 the Australians defeated England in a test match and thereafter consistently challenged England's earlier superiority. In the early years of the twentieth century rugby tours by South Africans, New Zealanders and Australians also became fairly regular events.

As whites settled in South Africa, they brought with them pastimes and sports from Europe. By the 1820s, hunting, horse racing and cricket were regular occurrences as the social trappings of elite English sport appeared on the South African scene. As elsewhere in the British Empire, hunts, horse races and cricket matches were social occasions where white officials and leading citizens could mingle and display their cultural superiority over the majority of residents as imperial culture sought to simultaneously impress and intimidate locals with its power and superiority. Sporting and social occasions were also about demonstrating the cultural superiority of white men, especially government officials, military officers and local landowing elites and entrepreneurs. Through sporting prowess and financial support, leading white men could demonstrate their cultural power.

Numerous national governing bodies for sport appeared in the 1890s and early 1900s, and by 1910 most major sports played by whites were organised on a national basis. The Football Association of South Africa, the South African Cyclists' Union and the South African Amateur Athletic Association formed in 1892, all white-only organisations. Swimming's national association appeared in 1899. Golf and tennis also emerged in the late nineteenth century and while these sports were also played by white women, they served to reinforce white power and difference as they also remained socially segregated. Tennis began in South Africa during the 1870s. In 1884 E. L. Williams became the first South African to appear in a Wimbledon final in the men's doubles, partnering an English player. The first national tennis championships were held in 1891. National associations were organised in tennis in 1903 and golf in 1909. Hockey was first played in 1899, introduced by British troops during the South African War of 1899 to1902.

One of South Africa's earliest local sporting heroes was Laurens Smitz Meintjes who became world cycling champion in the 1893. Meintjes was the first major South African sportsperson sent overseas to compete and his success led to calls for sporting tours to Britain in other sports.[9] Jan Hofmeyr, a member of the Cape Legislative Assembly, chaired a dinner in honour of Meintjes in Cape Town in 1893, demonstrating the official significance placed on international sporting success in the colonies. Hofmeyr eloquently stated what he thought the role of sport was in the imperial context and in the drive to unify southern African colonies into a national union:

> Sport has almost invariably been the pioneer of diplomacy in cementing the relationships and good understanding between Great Britain and her Colonies . . . the sporting associations of this country, which for the most part represent combinations of sportsmen throughout the various States, have set an example which politicians are all too slow to follow in the aim for a United South Africa.[10]

As in the late 1980s and early 1990s, sporting organisations in the 1880s and 1890s led the way in forming national associations prior to the political union of 1910. Clearly sport was one of the most important areas where national feelings were generated within the white societies of the Cape and Natal colonies, and the former Boer Republics and later colonies in the Transvaal and Orange Free State. Thus we can see that white South Africans took to the full range of British sports by the latter part of the nineteenth century. White South African sport developed in a similar fashion to sport in Britain and other settler societies, most closely resembling Australia and New Zealand.

Cricket rapidly became a prominent feature of imperial culture in South Africa and was one of the first sports linked closely with local political elites. It was initially imported by military personnel, administrators and settlers from Britain who arrived after 1820. In particular, the military was active in developing cricket in coastal towns. Cricket in South Africa grew as part of British imperialist ideology and increasingly its racist exclusivity. White cricket, and rugby soon thereafter, became entrenched in segregated schools and clubs (often based on old-boy groups) whose purpose was to demonstrate solidarity, superiority and separateness. Elitism and racism were the norm except for some rare mixing as part of celebrations on imperial holidays. The SARB founded in 1889 and the South African Cricket Association in 1890 – established to run the sports throughout South Africa – did not include any racially discriminatory clauses in their constitutions as no official considered that blacks would be a part of their associations. South African and imperial social customs already achieved sporting segregation.

Demonstrating imperial sporting links most clearly were annual cricket matches between the Mother Country and Colonial Born teams begun in 1864. Implicit in this contest was a deference to 'home' origins and the significance of cultural ties to Britain. Though not unique to South Africa, as such matches were common in Australia, New Zealand and elsewhere in the Empire, links to British culture were even more important in a setting where whites were surrounded by a large local population that white authorities linguistically constructed as 'uncivilised', different and ultimately inferior. Morrell shows how the small white population in Natal used rugby union and other imperial sports to culturally demarcate themselves from the overwhelming black majority.[11] The ability to appropriate and dispense British culture as the measure of social acceptability gave English-speaking whites and those they chose to include a real sense of cultural and moral power and superiority. As the twentieth century progressed, specific sports became synonymous with particular racial groups even though nearly all sports were played within the various social and cultural communities in South Africa. As a result, sporting practice and associated popular culture surrounding sport became distinct social signifiers within the country. Such signifiers have been difficult to remove even in the post-apartheid era.

Cricket was the most imperial of games, epitomising British culture, morality, manners and racism. The culture and discourses that surrounded cricket thus initially alienated Afrikaners as well as most blacks. In 1854, a match at the Cape involved 'Hottentots' (blacks) versus 'Boers' (Afrikaners), won by the former, but towards the end of the century, and in particular after the South African War, cricket found few adherents among Afrikaners. Cricket, as the epitome of Empire, was unlikely to attract those who considered themselves enemies of *die Engelse*. The apparent Afrikaner reluctance to take up cricket continued for several decades. Cricket thus became a symbol of the divisions among the whites of South Africa, as well as the separateness and exclusiveness of English-speaking whites from the rest of the population. However, after the National Party (NP) assumed power in 1948, cricket increasingly functioned as a means for the expression of white national unity, though many NP leaders continued to see the game as primarily one for English-speaking whites. For these reasons, cricket never achieved the same status as rugby during the apartheid years when Afrikaner nationalists ran the country. The relative insignificance of cricket to some Afrikaners is evidenced in a story about Prime Minister John Vorster in the late 1960s. He was told that *die Engelse* had lost three wickets for forty-two runs in the test between South Africa and England. Upon being given the information, Vorster replied, 'Hulle Engelse of ons Engelse?' ('Their English or our English?').[12]

Imbued with moral characteristics and an air of superiority, cricket was thought to be masterable by only those who had become 'civilised'.

In South Africa, the spatial dimensions of cricket also reinforced the exclusive discourse surrounding the game and its behaviour. Access to playing facilities was limited, particularly as segregation began to restrict blacks from playing on the same fields as whites. By the early 1900s, cricket represented sporting exclusivity, though middle-class blacks continued to play the game in segregated urban areas. Sports in general and cricket and rugby in particular were important means used to create social unity among English- speaking whites and to maintain social distance from the rest of the population.

Through the imperial connection and identifications with British imperial cultural practices, English-speaking whites always had an internationalist aspect to their national identity as South Africans within a larger British 'family' of nations. Many Afrikaners suspected that English-speaking whites were somehow less South African than them- selves and labelled them as less patriotic. English-speaking whites were assailed by Afrikaner nationalists for their flawed patriotism – they were not true South Africans but part of an overseas nation and a conduit for foreign capital and cultural interests. Cricket was labelled as one of these foreign activities, though ironically rugby, with nearly an equal imperial pedigree, was not. It is not clear, however, precisely why rugby was embraced by Afrikaners and not rejected like cricket. It appears that the rugby was never viewed as the imperial game par excellence nor was cricket as easily imbued with hearty colonial masculinist traits that could be transferred from discourses about the hearty masculine physicality of the frontier.

South African Rugby and the imperial connection

As with cricket, British officers and settlers also brought rugby to South Africa in the nineteenth century. The acknowledged founder of rugby in South Africa is Canon George Oglivie who became headmaster of Diocesan College, or Bishop's, in Cape Town in 1861 where he remained until 1885. A version of football began at Bishop's from this time, though the first recorded match took place on 23 August 1862. The *Cape Argus* on 21 August 1862 promoted the match:

FOOT-BALL
We are happy to find this fine old English school-game has been introduced amongst us. On Saturday next sides consisting of fifteen officers of the army and a like number of gentlemen in the civil service will open the Ball with a game on the race-course at Green Point.

> Of course this example will be speedily followed, and we shall have foot-
> ball treading closely on the likes of cricket and other imported manly games.[13]

Included in this first match was future Cape Prime Minister John X.
Merriman, his brother and other local notables. Even at this relatively
early stage, Afrikaners were playing football, as Adriaan van der Byl
kicked off to start the match. The imperial connection was evident,
however, at the outset as Governor Wodehouse of the Cape Colony was
in attendance. Bishop's and South African College, the leading Cape
private schools, also began to play against each other in the 1860s. The
version of football initially played resembled the game played at
Winchester School in England and many Winchester Old Boys played
important roles in starting what became rugby in South Africa. William
Henry Milton, an early England rugby union international[14] arrived in
Cape Town in 1878 and he persuaded Capetonian men that they were
playing an outmoded game. His recommendation that rugby's rules,
recently codified via the Rugby Football Union formed in 1871, be taken
up was followed.[15]

By 1879, the first two rugby union clubs, Hamilton and Villagers, had
been founded in Cape Town only a few years before the first Coloured
rugby clubs appeared. By 1883 rugby was strong enough in the Western
Cape for a governing body, the Western Province Rugby Football Union
(WPRFU), to be formed with a WPRFU organised club competition
beginning in the same year.[16] As with cricket, British regiments took an
early leading role in the spread of rugby beyond Cape Town, forming
clubs in the Eastern Cape and beyond in the late 1870s and 1880s.[17] On
31 May 1890 the first match was held at Newlands in Cape Town. As the
official history of the Newlands ground puts it:

> Special trains were arranged from Stellenbosch and Southern suburbs, and the
> Wynberg Military Camp band was in attendance. The Governor, Sir Henry
> Loch, and his entourage were accommodated in cane chairs.
> A crowd of about 2 400 turned up, which was considered excellent.[18]

As this passage shows, rugby was from its early history tied closely to
concepts of British civilisation, culture and imperial power. Similar to
England and Scotland, white rugby began as a private school and old-
boy club based clique. Of the twenty-three elite English-speaking schools
identified in a study by Hawthorne and Bristow, all have proud, long
and distinguished rugby histories.[19] Indeed, many religious figures such
as Oglivie, Walter Carey, later Bishop of Bloemfontein and H. B.
Bousfield, later Bishop of Pretoria, among others played prominent roles

in the diffusion of rugby throughout areas of white settlement in south-ern Africa.[20] But, as the quoted passage above also shows, rugby quickly developed a mass following among whites in the Western Cape. Although rugby began to be played by Afrikaners in Cape Town and Stellenbosch by the 1890s, they were rarely considered on equal terms with English-speaking whites when comments were made about sporting prowess. In this period, British attitudes towards Afrikaners were not much removed from those towards black Africans. As late as 1903, imperialist author and administrator John Buchan commented on Afrikaners and sport in harsh, and quite unfair, terms: 'It is worth while considering the Boer in sport, for it is there he is seen at his worst. Without tradition of fair play, soured and harassed by want and disaster, his sport became a matter of commerce, and he held no device unworthy . . . [The Afrikaners] are not a sporting race – they are not even a race of very skilful hunters.'[21]

Soon after the SARB was founded in 1889, international tours by British teams became regular occurrences. British teams toured South Africa in 1891, 1896 and 1903, with the South African War preventing tours between the latter two dates. British teams were initially success-ful winning all their matches in 1891 and only losing one test match to the South African team in 1896. Imperial links were frequently empha-sised during these tours. The 1891 British Isles team, consisting of twenty English and Scottish players, was greeted by a large group of officials, and supporters led a procession to the Royal Hotel where the team received flowers and ferns. The British team was treated to many smoking concerts, dinners, picnics and a formal ball at Government House. Cape Town newspapers discussed the tour in detail and gener-ated great public interest. In typical colonial reportage of matches against British teams, the *Cape Argus* reported that the tour would be a trial for South African rugby.[22] During the 1891 tour, Sir Donald Currie, diamond and gold magnate of Castle Mail Packets Ltd, which provided the sea link between South Africa and England, donated a trophy for an internal South African competition. The Currie Cup as it was to be called was first presented to the team that gave the British tourists the best game. Griqualand West was presented with the trophy that was sub-sequently used for the white South African provincial championships.[23] Currie had also presented a cup for inter-provincial white cricket in 1888.

The links between Empire and rugby in the 1890s can be best illus-trated by the Irish Banquet held in Cape Town on 5 September 1896 for the British Isles touring rugby team. The British tour took place at the time of the Jamieson Raid, an attempted uprising of British men in the Transvaal against the Afrikaner government there. At the banquet were leading members of the Cape government and other local and sporting officials as well as most of the players for the British and South African teams. Toasts were proposed to the Queen, the Governor and the Cape Ministry, and Sir James Sivewright, leading minister in the government, responded to the latter toast as the *Cape Argus* reported:

> They had had an awful year in South Africa. There had been a great deal to forgive and forget, and the sooner the better, but they were not going to forget the representative cricket and football teams that had visited South Africa (applause) and the visits would be enshrined in their memories. . . . The British race seemed to make football their prerogative and the parents of the game had sent out a team to teach the children, and Mr Hammond [British captain] would testify that they had learned their lesson well since the visit of the first team (cheers). The bull-dog characteristic of the race was called upon in the football field, and it did a great deal to make their men, not the game itself so much as the qualities which it encouraged (cheers). Such visits as the present one bound them to the Old Country with stronger bonds than ever.[24]

This passage demonstrates how sport could be used to divert attention from political strife, but more significantly just how important rugby and cricket tours were in cementing ties to Britain and the bonds of Empire and imperial culture. While the tone is deferential to Britain, it is clear that the local success was viewed as evidence of reaching a stage of cultural and even national maturity. Fittingly, South Africa won the fourth and final test on 5 September at Newlands 5–0 for their first ever victory over a British team. It was in this match that the South Africans first wore the green jerseys that were to become such a familiar sight in international rugby.

By 1903 the tide had shifted and South Africa began to dominate rugby encounters with British teams. The 1903 touring team to South Africa was part of the reconciliation process as British officials hoped to unite white South Africa as a nation under the imperial standard. South Africa defeated the British tourists of 1903 in the final test after the first two were drawn, thus winning its first international series seven years before the Union of South Africa created a country out of the four main white political entities in the region. South Africa was not to be beaten again in a rugby series until 1956 in New Zealand. South Africa's overwhelming success in international rugby can really be dated, however, from its tour of the British Isles in 1906. Although the 1903 team defeated the British tourists, it was success in the mother country that secured sporting reputations for colonial societies. South Africa's rugby successes in the British Isles in 1906 pre-dated their first official cricket test match win by twenty-nine years, thus assisting the development of rugby as the most significant national sport.[25] South Africa has been more successful in international rugby than in cricket, though cricket results in official matches in the 1960s and 1990s began to approach those of rugby.

The 1906–7 Springboks and white South African identity

The 1906–7 Springbok rugby tour was significant in helping to unite white South Africans, coming only four years after the South African War. The war fostered a deep animosity for the British on the part of Afrikaners as the British won the war largely due to their placing of Afrikaner women and children in concentration camps where 26,000 died. For the tour, however, both British Isles-descended players and Afrikaners were picked, with Paul Roos, an Afrikaner, as captain and Harold J. 'Paddy' Carolin as vice-captain. By this time, South African rugby had advanced dramatically and the Springboks were superior in organisation and physical ability in comparison with their British opponents.

The 1906 tour followed closely on the success of the first New Zealand All Black tour of Britain in 1905. The New Zealanders won all their matches except for a controversial test against Wales and were hailed as 'all conquering colonials' in the British press.[26] The South Africans were not quite as successful as the All Blacks, but they handily defeated Wales 11–0 in front of 50,000 spectators in Swansea. The British media, which had constructed the All Blacks as superior to British teams, did the same for the South Africans. After South Africa defeated Midland Counties 29–0, the *Daily Chronicle* stated that 'The Colonials have met the cream of the Midlands, and have made them look like thin skim milk'.[27] The South African team played an innovative style of rugby. They experimented with various formations and set plays and were the first national team to utilise the 3–4–1 scrum formation commonly used by nearly all future rugby teams. The 3–4–1 formation most probably appeared as a response to a 1905 rule change that did not allow forwards to put the ball back into the scrum with their feet. The South Africans also felt that the new formation would help them on wet grounds and thus used it in Britain in 1906–7. The Springboks also communicated in Afrikaans so that their signals could not be interpreted by opposing players.

Upon the conclusion of the tour, assessments in the British newspapers confirmed the overall dominance of the South Africans. The *Daily News* reported that there 'are many points of superiority left to the Old Country, but not as regards football'. The *Daily Express* went further in stating that at the time 'the English national genius is dormant, while the enterprising spirit of the Colonial never flags'. On a more hopeful note, the *Morning Post* echoed the emerging sentiments of many observers: 'The South Africans have demonstrated that the colonies are capable of rejuvenating the methods of the Motherland, and have shown that the race from which they spring is equal to ours in courage, chivalry and sportsmanship.'[28]

The 1906 South Africans also invented the nickname 'Springbokken' for themselves early on in the tour so that the British press would not invent one for them, according to captain Paul Roos.[29] The British media anglicised the name to 'Springboks' which has been used ever since to refer to the South African national team. The Springboks followed their 1906 successes with a tour in 1912–13 during which they defeated Scotland, Ireland, Wales, France and England. The victory over England was the first loss inflicted on them at Twickenham, opened in 1909. The Springboks went from strength to strength by not losing any home test match series played before 1974 and winning or drawing all of their series of tests both home and away from 1903 until 1956. After World War One, the number of Afrikaners playing rugby rose dramatically and in the 1930s and 1940s rugby began to slowly shift from a broader imperial focus to a South African nationalist focus, particularly as the Afrikaner Broederbond and the National Party began to target rugby as a central site for the expression of Afrikaner nationalism. We will return to these developments in chapter 4.

Already by the 1890s representative South African sides were mixed between English-speaking whites and Afrikaners. Initially, most Afrikaners were from Stellenbosch and Cape Town, but increasingly in the 1900s Afrikaner players also came from the Transvaal and Orange Free State. The University of Stellenbosch, as Albert Grundlingh shows, became the most significant training ground for top Afrikaner players.[30] In the 1890s, there was little to suggest, however, that an Afrikaner ethos of rugby had emerged to challenge British and imperial values. Indeed the rapid expansion of rugby among Afrikaners beyond the Western Cape areas of Cape Town and Stellenbosch was largely a result of rugby being played in prisoner-of-war camps during the South African War as Floris van der Merwe has shown.[31] Such challenges came later as Afrikaner nationalism developed in the 1930s and 1940s as a potent political, cultural and economic force in white South African society. Yet, the imperial connections lingered on long after rugby union's formative phase. In 1925 as part of the royal tour of the Prince of Wales (later Edward VIII) a special rugby match was held for the Prince played between the Universities of the Witwatersrand and Pretoria.[32] Indeed, for British sports officials the imperial connection was a vital part of sporting relations with South Africa. When the Afrikaner Nationalist government made South Africa a republic in 1961, South Africa was expelled not only from the Commonwealth but from most of its sporting institutions although the republic just managed to retain its place as a full member of the International Rugby Board (IRB).

Conclusion

Although the development of modern sport in South Africa took on many of the characteristics present in Britain and other English-speaking settler societies, South Africa became most rigid in its enforcement of racial segregation, which became one of the central organising principles in sport. In New Zealand, Maoris played regularly in provincial and national rugby teams, except when the All Blacks toured South Africa before 1970. Similar to the United States, blacks in South Africa were excluded from most sporting competitions in which whites participated by 1900. The imperial sporting model was a racist one. In the West Indies, no black player captained their cricket team on tour until 1960 and before that the captain was often the only white player in the team. Thus sport became one of the central cultural practices whereby white supremacy and difference were performed over time and in segregated spaces both in South Africa and throughout the Empire. White South African sports closely allied themselves with similar sporting organisations in Britain and in the white settler colonies of Australia and New Zealand. Thus, South African sport was initially infused with imperial ideologies of the power of the white and British race, of masculinity expressed through sporting prowess and of class distinctions learned through cultural performances such as sport. South Africa had one fundamental difference from other non-African settler societies, though. The white population never threatened to become a majority in South Africa whereas in Australasia and North America, whites overwhelmed native and black populations. As a result, attachment to cultural exclusivity remained more powerful in South Africa than elsewhere in the settler Empire. Despite the racist notions underpinning imperial sporting culture, black elites rapidly took to British sports such as rugby and cricket as they were also defined as markers of 'civilisation'. It is to the development of rugby and imperial sport in black communities that we turn in the next chapter before examining the emergence of rugby as a part of the Afrikaner nationalist project.

Notes

1 Though this could refer to any private school in the Empire based on the English public school model. Rugby developed into an intensely homophobic activity stressing aggressive masculinity while promoting group solidarity.
2 R. Morrell, 'Forging a ruling race: rugby and white masculinity in colonial Natal, c. 1870– 1910', in J. Nauright and T. J. L. Chandler (eds), *Making Men: Rugby and Masculine Identity* (London, Frank Cass, 1996); B. Spies, 'The imperial heritage: rugby and white English-speaking South Africa', in A. Grundlingh, A. Odendaal and B. Spies, *Beyond the Tryline: Rugby and South African Society* (Johannesburg, Ravan Press, 1995). This chapter is sketchy but provides an overview of the early history of rugby among English-speaking whites.
3 I. Difford, *The History of South African Rugby Football 1875–1932* (Cape Town, The Speciality Press of South Africa, 1933).
4 For discussion of the English public school model in South Africa, see P. Randall, *Little England on the Veld: The English Private School System in South Africa* (Johannesburg, Ravan, 1982).
5 J. Nauright, 'Sport, manhood and Empire: British responses to the New Zealand rugby tour of 1905'. *International Journal of the History of Sport*, 8:2 (1991), pp. 239–55; Nauright, 'Sport and the image of colonial manhood in the British mind: British physical deterioration debates and colonial sporting tours, 1878–1906', *Canadian Journal of History of Sport*, 23:2 (1992), pp. 54–71.
6 For a discussion of this process, see T. J. L. Chandler, 'The structuring of manliness and the development of rugby football at the public schools and Oxbridge, 1830–1880', in Nauright and Chandler, *Making Men*.
7 'Some tendencies of modern sport', *Quarterly Review*, 199:397 (January 1904), p. 127.
8 *The Times* (London), 10 October 1905.
9 F. J. G. van der Merwe, 'L. S. Meintjes: his impact on South African sport history', *Sporting Traditions*, 7:2 (1991), pp. 192–205.
10 Van der Merwe, 'L. S. Meintjes', p. 195.
11 Morrell, 'Forging a ruling race'.
12 D. Woods, *Black and White* (Dublin, Ward River Press, 1981), p. 46.
13 *Cape Argus* 21 August 1862.
14 England and Scotland began playing rugby union against each other only in the early 1870s.
15 P. Dobson, *Rugby in South Africa: A History 1861–1988* (Cape Town, South African Rugby Board, 1989), pp. 16–19.
16 Difford, *The History of South African Rugby*, pp. 12–13.
17 Difford, *The History of South African Rugby*, pp. 12–14.

18 Western Province Rugby Football Union, *A Century at Newlands* (Cape Town, Western Province Rugby Football Union, 1990), p. 1.

19 P. Hawthorne and B. Bristow, *Historic Schools of South Africa: An Ethos of Excellence* (Cape Town, 1993).

20 Also see the discussion of early rugby, schools and the imperial heritage in Spies, 'The imperial heritage'.

21 Quoted in R. Archer and A. Bouillon, *The South African Game: Sport and Racism* (London, Zed Press, 1982), p. 18.

22 C. Greyvenstein, *Springbok Rugby: An Illustrated History* (London, New Holland, 1995), p. 11.

23. As a point of historical accuracy, some suggest that the Currie Cup was given to Griqualand West who then generously donated it to the SARB. Currie's instructions were, however, that the trophy was to be for an internal competition, see Greyvenstein, *Springbok Rugby*, p. 12.

24 *Cape Argus* 7 September 1896, p. 6.

25 Though a South African team did defeat an MCC side at Lord's in 1894 by eleven runs. This was the first cricket team from South Africa to venture to England.

26 Nauright, 'Sport, manhood and Empire'.

27 *Daily Chronicle* (London), 29 September 1906.

28 Quoted in L. Laubscher and G. Nieman, *The Carolin Papers: A Diary of the 1906–07 Springbok Tour* (Pretoria, Rugbyana Publishers, 1990), p. 212. This quotes a South African tour correspondent's review of the English daily press on 2 January 1907.

29 A Springbok is a member of the antelope family and is common in southern Africa.

30 A. Grundlingh, 'Playing for power?: rugby, Afrikaner nationalism and masculinity in South Africa, *c.* 1900–*c.*1970', in Nauright and Chandler, *Making Men*.

31 F. J. G. van der Merwe, 'Rugby in the prisoner-of-war camps during the Anglo Boer War, 1899–1902', paper presented to the Football and Identities International Conference, University of Queensland, Brisbane, 21–23 March 1997.

32 Difford, *The History of South African Rugby*, p. 615.

Chapter 3

Black rugby and sports, sporting ideologies and racial politics

Sport among the black population in South Africa has a long history despite frequent white pronouncements to the contrary. It is impossible in this context to understand the development of sport in black communities without some sense of general historical processes. Two factors were crucial in the emergence of black sporting organisations and competitions in South Africa. The first of these were the mission stations founded by various groups of missionaries from Britain, continental Europe and the USA and the second was the process of urbanisation unleashed by the discovery of diamonds at Kimberley in 1867 and gold on the Witwatersrand and the founding of Johannesburg in 1886. In Cape Town, an established mixed race or Coloured population also existed and it became one of the early centres for sporting organisation among black South Africans.

As industralisation and economic expansion progressed in the late nineteenth and early twentieth centuries, educated black South African men were employed in many clerical and some professional positions. These men began to form a cultural elite tied to the ideologies surrounding concepts of Western civilisation promoted by the British and other Western missionaries. Indeed, these men promoted an ideology of respectability based on relative civilisation defined through British cultural attributes such as afternoon tea, cricket, rugby and other British sports, the reading of classical British literature and Christianity (though the latter was not adopted by many well-educated Muslim Coloureds in Cape Town). In this chapter we discuss the emergence of black rugby in the context of black elites adopting British sporting and attendant cultural practices, followed by a case study of the cultural centrality of Coloured rugby in Cape Town and the segregated system in which black rugby and other sporting associations were forced to operate in the first ninety years of the twentieth century.

Despite the evidence of black sporting clubs and associations existing for decades, little has been written on the history of black sport either for the popular market or by academics. Several studies of black sport appeared in the 1980s and early 1990s that focused on the emergence of sport among urban elites in Kimberley, Johannesburg and Vereeniging, and a recent book on rugby discusses some of the history of black rugby.[1] Beyond this, however, we have little understanding of the rich history of black sporting organisations that operated during the segregation and apartheid eras. The predominant white South African attitude towards black sport in general centres on beliefs that blacks have not played sport, at least Western style sport, for nearly as long as whites, or that blacks have their own sporting culture centred on soccer and boxing that is very different from that of whites. In a representative and classic essentialist statement made in 1994, Springbok rugby hero Uli Schmidt stated that rugby was not in the culture of blacks and it was not natural for them to play, rather they should play soccer.[2] In a recent chapter discussing some of the history of black rugby, Andre Odendaal reports how Hannes Marais, convenor of the Springbok selection panel in 1995, suggested in 1971 that 'The Coloured populations [*sic*] does not seem very interested in sport. They do not play much rugby and cricket'. Additionally, Dawid de Villiers, former Springbok captain, National Party minister and a cabinet minister in the initial post-apartheid government of national unity, said in 1980: 'Don't forget that the Blacks have really known western sports [only] for the last ten years . . . they have not reached the same standard [as whites]'.[3] Even in the international academic literature, statements about blacks not having the opportunity to play white sports have appeared thus assisting in the perpetuation of the myth of low sporting participation among Africans. Stoddart, in an otherwise excellent article on imperial sport, argues that given the 'concern with reconciling Boer and Briton, black and coloured communities had few if any opportunities to play rugby union'.[4]

Such white perceptions contrast sharply with the reality of black sporting experience and support for sport in black communities. In many areas of the Western and Eastern Cape in particular, rugby has been immensely popular for many decades and for *more than a century* in some areas. Gassan Emeran, a former school principal and cricketer, stated that in District Six and the Bo-Kaap, the two main Coloured residential areas within the central areas of Cape Town up to 1970,[5] 'whenever you meet people it was just rugby, there was nothing else it was just, rugby, rugby, rugby. That was their life – rugby. They talked of nothing else but rugby, that is why they are very knowledgeable.' Furthermore, 'rugby was the game that everybody played. Even some girls played rugby with the boys in their younger years.'[6] 'Meneer' Effendi, a long-time rugby administrator, also relates the significance of rugby in the Coloured community of Cape Town: 'each club had a huge following we played our matches at the Green Point track on the Saturday and on the Sunday – you had to witness a Sunday match to be able to get that feeling, to see the families come with their picnic baskets and whatever, it is a day.'[7] As Odendaal puts it: 'Contrary to general knowledge, black South Africans have a long, indeed remarkable, rugby and sporting history.'[8] Thus, a paradox presents itself to us, on the one hand white ignorance of black rugby and wider sporting cultures has served to legitimate the position of whites while justifying the slow pace of reform, on the other, we have a long history that has been marginalised through racist divisions in society and lack of outlets for the production of black sporting histories.

This paradox is not surprising given that most South African whites into the 1990s only came into contact with blacks as workers, and few whites have ever ventured into a black township. As a result, most whites have little direct cultural links with blacks and have not played sport with or against them until very recently, if at all. A geography of mental separation pervades South African society where whites visualise blacks away in out-of-sight townships and either forget about what they might be doing in their leisure time or assume that they are drinking and committing crime as the media and their education system taught them to think during the apartheid era.

While white ignorance has been one problem affecting black sport, blacks in South Africa encountered political interference in their attempts to maintain and improve their sporting opportunities throughout the segregation and apartheid eras. Interference came from white sporting authorities and from the state. Thus black sport has faced marginalisation on a number of significant fronts. As a result, a comprehensive analysis of the history of black rugby and other sporting development is not possible. Our aim in this chapter is not to attempt a broad survey but, through the richness of some of the available material, to partially reconstruct and discuss the development of rugby in segregated black communities and the political ramifications generated by these segregated sporting structures.

While segregation imposed by white sporting organisations and government policies did much to promote divisions in sport, social divisions also were generated within black communities based on religion, ethnicity, language or residential patterns. In Cape Town, two distinct rugby unions emerged among Coloureds, one that was predominantly Muslim and one that banned Muslims until the 1960s. Gender differences were also crucial and urban black sport became closely linked with notions of urban black masculinity. Black women on average have had far fewer opportunities to play sport than their white counterparts. As modern forms of sports and urban culture began to develop among whites in the latter half of the nineteenth century, blacks also became exposed to British cultural forms that included sport. If we are to understand adequately the position of many ANC and leading black sporting officials in the new South Africa, then we need to understand the historical, social and political development of black sport.

Missions, racial ideologies and British sport among urban black elites

By the 1830s, mission stations began to appear in present-day South Africa, particularly in the Eastern Cape region coming under British control, where some Africans were educated to European moral and social standards. Brian Willan, in his biographical study of Sol Plaatje, an early African nationalist leader, describes the process whereby one group of Africans, the Barolong, came to be on mission stations and how some like Plaatje's family came to be educated by missionaries into a European world-view. When missionaries first encountered the Barolong they met with resistance from chiefs. African chiefs and kings sometimes used the presence of missionaries to try and protect themselves and their people from dispossession, but most did not want a permanent missionary presence that might ultimately undermine their authority. Many early converts were refugees following the disruptions of the *mfecane*, a regional conflict over land that spread across southern Africa during the 1820s and 1830s. Others were social outcasts from their own societies. A number of Barolong people went to Thaba Nchu in the present day Orange Free State during the 1830s to seek refuge and came under the influence of missionaries there.

The concepts of civilisation as espoused by missionaries went hand-in-hand with the expression of British imperial power as British influence over southern Africa spread. White officials and missionaries held out the notion of 'civilisation', rather than solely race or colour, as the criteria for acceptance into wider Cape colonial society. The Cape colony developed a non-racial franchise by the end of the nineteenth century, though with such strict provisions that only a handful of Africans could qualify for the vote. The most successful area of missionary endeavour was in the Eastern Cape region in the areas near East London, Queenstown and King William's Town. As mission-educated Africans moved to towns and cities, they clung to the concepts of civilisation, Christianity and British culture as the determinants of social position and worth and the only viable option for personal and social improvement. Rapid expansion of mission endeavours took place between the 1860s and 1900s. In 1865 there were 2,827 students in mission schools, but by 1885 this number had risen dramatically to 15,568 in 700 schools. British sports and recreational activities were important at these schools as missionaries deemed African traditional recreational culture to be 'incompatible with Christian purity of life'.[9]

White missionaries initially used cricket in their attempts to inculcate the concepts surrounding respectability through sport to an emerging black middle class. Throughout the British Empire, cricket became a crucial cultural activity that helped to define a supposedly civilised man, and black middle-class males adopted cricket and its cultural trappings as part of the adoption of many aspects of British civilisation. The adoption of British culture set apart Western-educated black men from the majority of blacks in southern Africa. By the middle of the nineteenth century mission-educated blacks were participating in a wide variety of British cultural activities. Organised sport, including cricket, rugby, tennis, croquet and soccer, was particularly well developed in the Eastern Cape by the 1860s. In 1862, John Shedden Dobie reported that Africans living on a farm near Queenstown played cricket with the white farm owner. The first known African cricket club was founded in Port Elizabeth in 1869. By 1887 black sporting participation in the Eastern Cape was widespread enough for *Imvo Zabantsundu* (an African newspaper based in King William's Town) to have a section devoted to sport.[10] From the late nineteenth century onwards, the Eastern Cape became a centre of black political organisation as educated black men formed a variety of associations. Many of these political leaders also involved themselves in sporting clubs as players and administrators. As a result, strong ties emerged between black political organisations and sport. In the Eastern Cape links between politics and sport remained strong throughout the segregation and apartheid periods. In the 1970s, Steve Biko and other Black Consciousness leaders made speeches at sporting matches often hidden among groups of fans to avoid police detection. The United Democratic Front also used similar strategies in the 1980s.

Links between politics and sport were not unique to the Eastern Cape, however. Throughout many areas of Africa, sporting clubs provided the initial location for interaction between different groups of African elites within a colony as educated Africans gravitated to administrative, professional and educational posts in colonial capitals and large regional towns. John Iliffe in his history of Tanganyika argues that the earliest African urban political organisations there developed from within the soccer clubs in Dar-es-Salaam in the 1930s.[11] This pattern recurred throughout sub-Saharan Africa as colonial officials encouraged soccer and other sporting clubs and recognised sporting clubs as legal urban African organisations. The dominant thinking in official colonial and missionary circles was that sport provided a moralistic way to occupy the leisure time of newly urbanised Africans, which would limit the possibilities of social and political unrest. Ossie Stuart points out, however, that soccer teams often became the focus of protests and strikes in colonial Zimbabwe (then known as Southern Rhodesia) in the 1940s. He goes further to state that soccer 'played a key role in providing one of the few avenues available anywhere in colonial Africa to social mobility and high status. It should thus be unsurprising that there was no boundary between political action and sport' among urban black leaders.[12] The South African case was no different. Yet, despite its role in galvanising local elites and urbanising masses in protest against colonial rule, sport in Africa after independence has proved to be a conservative institution closely linked to new post-colonial power structures, not unlike modern sport in most other societies and no different from sports administration in post-apartheid South Africa as we shall see.

While white missionaries promoted sport and men among the black elite took to sport as part of a process of cultural transformation, missionaries and mine owners promoted sport in their efforts to moralise the leisure time of the majority of blacks moving into urban centres or who worked as migrants on the mines.[13] As in urban centres across colonial Africa, mine owners sought social activities that might prevent the emergence of serious social unrest, mass strikes and unionisation.

While missionaries and white officials played key roles in the establishment of British sporting practices among Africans, black sporting organisations soon emerged run by Africans at local, provincial and national levels. Alan Cobley argues that there was a clear divide in black sports between elite and mass sporting forms. For the elite the mission experience was crucial. Cobley states that 'graduates of mission institutions in towns formed themselves into teams and practised the skills they had learned at school as much from a desire to emphasise their social advantages, class position and consciousness, as for the joy of the games itself'.[14] In this manner, black sport differed little in its social and cultural context from white sport in late nineteenth-century Europe.

Urban black elites, respectability and sport

Missionaries offered the possibility of achieving civilised status to blacks who became Christian and went through mission education. As blacks moved to urban areas to seek better employment opportunities, they had to settle in racially and not culturally segregated areas and construct new patterns of social existence different from those that had operated in rural areas. Within racially segregated residential areas, however, blacks with some financial resources could settle in some relatively better places than the many urban slums. Those from the better-off peasant and share-cropping areas of the Transvaal and the Orange Free State, for example, often moved to the freehold townships of Sophiatown and Alexandra near Johannesburg between 1912 and the 1930s. These townships offered the possibility of land ownership and were relatively uncrowded until the 1930s. Many of the initial migrants came to cities to accumulate resources for marriage, or to buy property and houses in rural areas, though some chose to become permanently urbanised. It became most pre-stigious to have a job in Johannesburg. Once migrants married they often tried to settle in Sophiatown or Alexandra, which had more respectable reputations than Johannesburg's inner-city slums.

Research on social and early political organisation in Johannesburg and Kimberley demonstrates that the impact of mission education was strong in the establishment of an urban black elite.[15] Attracted to skilled positions such as clerks in these rapidly expanding cities, these educated Africans and Coloureds adopted an ideology of respectability based on British high culture that set them apart from the majority of African migrant workers and poor whites who also flocked to the cities in the wake of the mineral revolution, drought and reorganisation of land-use in the countryside.

By the early 1900s, the African educated elite had mobilised itself into political organisations, which the South African Native Affairs Commission noted 'were taking an active and intelligent interest in polit-ical affairs'.[16] This group developed newspapers to promote greater communication about social, political, economic and cultural events that affected their interests. Odendaal shows that many early political organ-isations focused on local issues and had short lifespans, however, they were 'symptomatic of an ever-increasing African interest in political affairs and organisation at grassroots level'.[17] In addition to these local political organisations, many teachers' associations, social clubs, financial self-help groups and sporting clubs also appeared during this period. In Kimberley, Africans formed the South African Improvement Society in 1895. The society promoted the use of the English language and its very name suggested the notion of moving to some higher state of being, of becoming something 'civilised' or 'respectable'. At one of its early meetings, the society heard a lecture entitled 'Civilisation and its Advantages to African Races'.[18] In Cape society, the use of the English language was central in the civilising process as was the adoption of British attitudes and cultural activities including cricket and rugby. Stoddart discusses the way that British culture was transferred to colonial elites though 'informal authority systems' such as the English language that became 'not simply a conveyer of information between otherwise differing cultural groups, it was a medium for the exchange of moral codes and social attitudes. Attaining command of the "proper" English language, accent as well as vocabulary and syntax, became the goal of innumerable colonial peoples.'[19] Virtually every black sporting association used English as the official language for meetings, even in cases where the first language of members was Afrikaans or Zulu.

The role of sport in the cultural politics of identity among the black male elite is clear from a late nineteenth-century example. In August 1896 a celebration was held for two men who had been accepted to attend Wilberforce University in the USA. One of the men, H. C. Msikinya, listed his social accomplishments including his role as President of the Come Again Lawn Tennis Club, Secretary to the Eccentrics Cricket Club, member of the Rovers Rugby Football Club and member of the South African Improvement Society. Significantly, three of the four societies were sporting ones and included the British and supposedly cultured sports of tennis, cricket and rugby. By 1900, imperial sport was significant in attempts by the African elite to establish their civilised credentials both in terms of their own community and in relation to whites. Every man who wanted to be known in the black establishment in Kimberley sought to be an office bearer in the Duke of Wellington or Eccentrics Cricket Clubs whether they actually played cricket or not according to Willan. He describes how Sol Plaatje became Joint Secretary of the Eccentrics Cricket Club even though he had not learned to play cricket on the German mission station where he grew up. Willan states further that it was in the company of cricket club office bearers where Plaatje internalised and subsequently retained the qualities and values embodied in cricket. In 1930 Plaatje dedicated one of his translations of Shakespeare to his friend Arthur Motlala, stating that Motlala was 'a loyal friend, a splendid cricketer, and an able Penman'.[20] The role of sport in the lives of elite blacks is evidenced in Mweli Skota's *African Yearly Register* published in 1932. Many of the African personalities included by Skota listed sport among their principal leisure activities. Additionally, Skota obviously selected some of the personalities because of their sporting prowess. Of those who mentioned sport, the most popular sports were cricket (44.5 per cent), tennis (30 per cent) and football (22.4 per cent).[21]

By the mid-1880s there were several well-established African cricket clubs in the Eastern Cape playing in regular competitions. The first African newspaper, *Imvo Zabantsundu*, founded in 1884, helped establish the importance of these competitions through regular reporting of matches. By 1887 the newspaper had a sporting editor and many advertisements targeted cricket and cricket clubs. Not only did African teams play against each other, but some interracial matches also began to take place in the 1880s. In 1885, a black team beat the local whites at King William's Town, and in the same year blacks from Port Elizabeth defeated the whites of Cradock.

Black sport developed securely within the imperial context. Matches between whites and blacks were a feature of imperial public holidays in particular in the late nineteenth century. Black cricket clubs frequently had imperial-sounding names that often emulated those used by white clubs in Britain or South Africa. This was part of the process of demonstrating respectability and attachment to imperial culture. The ideology of respectability was crucial in the aspirations of middle-class blacks. Colonial and later South African governments would only converse with those whom they believed behaved in a European manner, even if they denigrated such blacks in discussions with other whites. In Kimberley, a Christmas Day cricket match was the highlight of the local annual social calendar for the black elite. This match, like white matches, celebrated imperial culture, and included music played by bands and was attended by leading locals.

The paternalistic and long-term assimilationist cultural approach characteristic of imperial and Cape liberalism in the nineteenth century slowly gave way to a more segregationist approach that wanted to limit the ability of blacks to compete with whites in wider society. As some blacks became highly educated, concerns about the overall competitiveness of blacks led to more segregationist policies. Such notions were promoted especially by Afrikaner leaders as many poor Afrikaners moved from the countryside to the city in the first two decades of the 1900s.

By the early twentieth century, social institutions were adapted to play a role not only of social control but also for purposes of exclusivity. White officials increasingly thought that the proper place for blacks was as labourers and servants. Blacks were progressively consigned to inferior social, political and economic positions by exclusion from the vote, land ownership, commercial opportunities and complete cultural segregation. In this climate, it is not surprising that the little inter-racial sport played in the late nineteenth century rapidly disappeared in the early 1900s. Despite being excluded from sporting competitions with whites on the basis of race, however, urban African elites continued to organise their own competitions in cricket, rugby, soccer, boxing and other sports and these competitions grew and flourished despite frequent opposition from municipal officials, the police and the segregation and apartheid states. One of the best documented cases of sporting development was that of coloured rugby in Cape Town. Although records are not complete, association documents and newspaper accounts, coupled with interview material, allow for a resonable understanding of the cultural centrality of rugby and the political contexts in which rugby developed both at local and national levels.

Coloured rugby and the politics of identity in Cape Town

District Six and the Bo-Kaap became South Africa's first real working-class areas. When the slaves were freed by the British officials in 1838, more than 5,000 needed homes. Most of the Muslims, mainly of Malay origin, settled in what was later to become the Bo-Kaap or the Malay Quarter. Others moved to the opposite side of Cape Town beyond Roeland Street at the edge of the central business district in the area that became known as District Six. Overcrowding affected the district by the time the Cape Town City Council officially named the area in 1867 as the sixth district of the Cape Town municipality. In 1900, during the South African War, a concerted building programme began in District Six, providing the physical structure for the community. The official population figures for District Six stood at 22,440 in 1936; 28,377 in 1946; but by the early 1950s the population had passed 40,000.[22] Don Pinnock describes District Six aptly, as it was known for the 'ingenuity, novelty and enterprise of its residents, engaged in this mode of small-scale production and services. By day it hummed with trade, barter and manufacture, and by night it offered the "various pleasures of conviviality or forgetfulness".[23]

The two main areas of Coloured settlement in Cape Town developed their own distinct, albeit related, communities. Muslim and non-Muslim culture differed in religious terms, yet the groups developed many common cultural practices in music and sport. Rugby became the dominant winter sport by the early 1900s, though interest in soccer began to grow in the 1920s. Male schoolteachers promoted rugby in particular and viewed it as an ideal means of teaching discipline and for generating social cohesion.[24] Such promotion of rugby union is not dissimilar to other areas where the game was actively encouraged in schools, though it would be wrong to assume that because whites played rugby in their schools that coloureds merely copied white sporting structures and cultural values attached to sport. Rugby emerged as a manly and character-forming game among Cape Town's elite Coloured schools, developing from the influence of British missionaries combined with the harsh realities of everyday life in the cramped areas of District Six and the Bo-Kaap. The notion of respectability was a strong influence on the urban African elite; however, in Cape Town this was also infused with concepts of respectable behaviour and self-discipline that stemmed from Muslim culture and the teachings of the *Koran*.

Rugby and cricket were the first sports to be organised among blacks in Cape Town, with soccer and boxing following several decades later. The first known Coloured rugby clubs appeared in Cape Town in 1886, three years before the formation of the SARB as a national governing body for white rugby. Two rugby unions emerged in the Cape Town area, which administered two distinct competitions, the Western Province Coloured Rugby Football Union (WPCRFU) founded in 1886 and the City and Suburban Rugby Union (CSRU) founded in 1898. These two organisations reflected religious distinctions that operated within the Coloured communities of Cape Town as some Coloureds were Muslim while others were Christian, or at least non-Muslim. Rugby dominated the Coloured sport scene in Cape Town from the 1880s through to the late 1960s and was an integral part of local culture and the display of masculinity through physical performance. Some rugby clubs gained reputations from their use of intimidating tactics while the Western Province representative team of the WPCRFU was also feared because of its physicality and psychological ability to frighten opponents before matches even started. The bulk of the WPCRFU players were Muslim, though non-Muslims were not excluded and indeed were welcomed into clubs. Perhaps there was more to muscular Islam than to muscular Christianity within the Coloured rugby-playing community.[25] One reason for the WPCRFU retaining a reputation for tough and robust play is that the base of its clubs remained in the inner-city, predominantly working-class areas of District Six and the Bo-Kaap while the centre of CSRU activity increasingly moved to suburban Cape Town by the 1950s and 1960s. District Six and the Bo-Kaap were tightly knit communities where people lived in close proximity and where survival for working-class and middle-class men often meant becoming tough through the development of physical abilities. School teachers recognised the need for such toughness hence their encouragement of rugby playing among boys.

Five important Coloured rugby clubs were founded in 1886 in Cape Town. Four of these clubs, Roslyn, Good Hopes, Violets and Arabian College, came together to found the WPCRFU. A fifth club, Wanderers, became the prime mover behind a second union formed in 1898, the CSRU. Several clubs that formed in the late 1880s and 1890s did not join the WPCRFU and joined with Wanderers to found the CSRU, a union that excluded Muslims until the 1960s.[26] One incident relating to CSRU official attitudes towards Muslims is illuminating. In 1931, the CSRU investigated the alleged identity of a player on one of its affiliated clubs who was reportedly seen wearing a fez – the colourful red hats worn frequently by Muslim men in Cape Town. After a detailed investigation that included exmaination of a birth certificate and the interviewing of several people, it was discovered that the player in question was indeed of Muslim background. He was summarily dismissed from playing in the CSRU and his club repremanded.[27] This incident illustrates white policies were not the only factors in the creation and maintenance of social divisions through the cultural practice of rugby in South Africa, but that historical agents in local communities also profoundly shaped local rugby cultures.

The other founding clubs of the CSRU were California (1888); Perseverance (1889); Thistles (1891); Woodstock Rangers (1892); and Retreat (1898). Primrose joined in 1901, Progress in 1906 and Universal in 1931 to form the core of CSRU clubs until the 1960s. The CSRU also developed some links with rugby teams and associations in the Boland area east of Cape Town. The WPCRFU was well connected with the national South African Coloured Rugby Football Board (SACRFB), founded in Kimberley in 1897. The WPCRFU was very successful in the national provincial level Rhodes Cup competitions. The Rhodes Cup, offered for competition on a similar basis to the Currie Cup for whites, was a pinnacle of Coloured rugby competition, but due to the expense of long-distance travel and other factors, the tournament was not held every year. The fragile nature of black sporting associations is evidenced in the problems faced by the WPCRFU as it nearly collapsed in the early 1930s, with only Roslyn and Violets surviving from the original clubs. Several clubs emerged in the 1930s, however, to revitalise the union. These clubs included Young Stars (1928); Orange Blossoms (1931); Caledonian Roses (1934); and Buffaloes (1936). Other clubs in the competition by 1940 were Hamediahs, Evergreens, Watsonias, Young Ideas and Leeuwendale. These WPCRFU clubs were all based in the Bo-Kaap and District Six.

District Six was a vibrant area of cultural activities, with sports playing an important part in local culture. Of the sports played, rugby was the most prominent in the District as well as in the Bo-Kaap. Gassan Emeran, a school principal from the Bo-Kaap and former cricketer, states that culture, politics and even life itself revolved around rugby and for the Islamic majority of District Six and the Bo-Kaap, rugby was the 'second religion'.[28] Effendi argues that the 'non-white community as such was a very sport loving community' and that rugby 'brought the whole community together'.[29] In addition to organised rugby, many matches took place on Sundays, which the media did not cover. Some Sunday teams eventually decided to play more formally, which led to the entry of additional clubs into WPCRFU competitions in the 1930s and 1940s. These Sunday matches allowed far greater numbers of men from District Six and the Bo-Kaap to participate in a physical team sport where masculine attributes could be displayed on a less organised and routinised level. Thus we can see that a vibrant and widespread Coloured rugby culture had emerged in Cape Town by the middle of the century.

While participation was an important element in rugby's cultural significance among Coloureds in Cape Town, spectating was even more broadly inclusive as it included women and children. Informants interviewed by Nauright discussed the community element of the game, though this was clearly a community where men dominated. Men controlled most public spaces. Many rugby club activities were homosocial, though clubs raised money through dances that involved women in club activities. Matches between the WPCRFU and the CSRU drew the largest crowds whether played at the WPCRFU home ground at Green Point Track or the CSRU grounds. The CSRU rarely defeated the WPCRFU though often there was little difference in ability between top players in the two unions. Gassan Emeran suggests that the WPCRFU was more successful because they could intimidate the CSRU, with WPCRFU players starting the psychological process months in advance. Players from both unions worked together and met each other outside the rugby arena so the intimidation was purely linked to rugby, unlike the periodic violence that accompanied some club rugby.[30] Although divisions existed, rugby enabled men who played and watched it to generate a sense of respect for each other that extended beyond any religious differences, and the presence of women and children generated a vibrant community atmosphere around the sport. Thus rugby aided in the formation of cross-religious group identity. For men, this identity was based on violent physicality as displayed on the rugby field, though union officials frowned upon violence beyond accepted parameters and punished offenders, thus maintaining a sense of respectability and discipline around the game.

District Six increasingly came under the influence of gangsters and protection rackets in the 1940s and 1950s and some of these linked themselves closely with rugby clubs. In particular, the dominant gang of the 1950s, the Globe Gang, strongly supported Roslyn, the most powerful and oldest club in the WPCRFU competition. Clubs from both the WPCRFU and CSRU congregated on different street corners for team meetings to announce team selections and to discuss and analyse previous match performances. Roslyn, for example, met in front of the Globe Furnishing Company, side-by-side with the Globe Gang which also met there.[31] Pinnock describes how the Globe Gang came into being in the 1940s. As greater numbers of people moved into the District from other areas, the incidence of petty theft by young males increased. In response to this threat, the sons of shopkeepers began to meet outside the Globe Furnishing Company in Hanover Street opposite the Star Bioscope. They began by smashing a 'tax-racket' at the cinema where patrons were forced to pay a penny to youths before entering. Leaders of the Globe Gang were bricklayers, hawkers and painters. The core of the gang formed around the Ishmail family, one of whom was a City Councillor.[32] Pinnock points out that as more people moved into the District, 'the Globe was an organisation that sought to assert and maintain the control of the more wealthy families and the hawkers'.[33] According to one Globe member:

> The Globe hated the skollie[34] element in town, like the people who robbed the crowds on [celebrations] or when there were those marches in town with the Torch Commando or Cissy Gool's singsong [demonstration] outside Parliament buildings. Mikey and the boys would really bomb out the skollie element when they robbed the people then. They tore them to ribbons.[35]

The Globe Gang had a close relationship with the police who counted on the gang to help control the District. The Globe soon became a protection racket with all in their area having to pay allegiance. Pinnock explains that by 1950 'the Globe was controlling extortion, blackmail, illicit buying of every kind, smuggling, shebeens, gambling, and political movements in the District'.[36] Slowly, prison elements took control of the gang throughout the 1950s and more direct acts of intimidation, theft and murder became a regular part of Globe activities. Globe influence also affected rugby as the gang was a strong supporter of the Roslyn club.

While Roslyn's specific ties to the Globe Gang are not entirely clear, the club had a reputation for its fans, including Globe members, intimidating referees and opposing players. Former Montrose players state that when they played for Young Stars they had trouble finding referees for matches against Roslyn as 'the referees were frightened because Roslyns must win, if Roslyns doesn't win, it's a fight because they got their stones and their chains ready and their big swords ready that means they're going to attack'.[37] In one game between Stars and Roslyn, Rajab Benjamin, a founder of the Montrose club in the WPCRFU, scored near the end of the match and Stars only had to kick the conversion for a win. Benjamin says he knew the chains would come out when he made the kick since the Roslyn's fans knew they would lose. 'When we passed the Globe corner and they had their table decorated because they were winning the trophy back this year'.[38] Some fans had pangas and chains and Benjamin readied for a quick escape after the match. Montrose players argued that it was mainly Roslyn and their fans who behaved this way, asserting that they had to win partly because they had all the delegates in the union. Roslyn supplied many important and widely respected administrators, such as 'Meneer' Adams and 'Meneer' Effendi, both school teachers and long-serving Roslyn and WPCRFU administrators.

The links between gangs and rugby are recorded by the writer Richard Rive. Rive recounts the story of one gang, the Jungle Boys, and their links with rugby in his autobiographical novel of life in District Six, *Buckingham Palace, District Six*. Three gang leaders formed the front-row of the Young Anemones Rugby Football Club's first team. Rive states that they 'practised in Trafalgar Park and played hard and dirty. They turned up regularly with their team to fulfil fixtures but these seldom materialised because most of the teams they were scheduled to play would rather forfeit the match than meet the Jungle Boys head on'.[39]

Rough, intimidating play was a feature of District Six rugby, at least among some clubs. Roslyn had a reputation for toughness among WPCRFU clubs, but the WPCRFU also had a general reputation for playing hard, intimidating rugby. Given the social conditions in District Six and to a lesser degree in the Bo-Kaap, this tough style of play should not be surprising, even though many leading rugby players tended to be from better off families of the petty bourgeoisie. Rajab Benjamin relates that violent play was part of the tactics of rugby, but that any roughness or violence stayed on the field of play and did not continue outside the ground after a match. He explains how he stopped Eastern Province one year in the Rhodes Cup when Western Province were being over-run by an Eastern Province winger:

> I said to our captain, you must make a change man . . . we gonna lose. So he ask me what can we do? So I say the only thing you can do is change me from my position . . . I was a loose forward and I went to go and play in his posi-tion. The first time he come past, the second time he's gone off the field, so there are no more tries coming from their side . . . It shows you the tactics you must use – you must use your brains.[40]

Here it appears that using your brains meant figuring out a way to stop the opposition in any way necessary to achieve the desired result. In this context, the use of trickery was an important part of playing the game. Trickery involved a range of intimidatory tactics, some of which were viewed in white rugby circles as unacceptable. The differences in accept-able on-field behaviour led to a number of problems after rugby unity in 1992, particularly in the Western Cape, as the provincial tribunal has been faced with different perceptions of acceptable violence among players.

Evidence from the local newspapers aimed at the coloured market, the *Cape Standard* and the *Cape Sun*, from the 1930s and 1940s suggests that violent play on the field occurred regularly. Despite this, CSRU records show that the union took a hard line with those found guilty of rough play, with suspensions ranging from a couple of matches to two years. The WPCRFU also suspended players for exceedingly rough play, but documents do not exist to establish whether there was a consistent policy of punishment. What is clear is that a culture of rough play was an accepted part of the game, though there were limits to the levels of vio-lence tolerated. It is not clear, however, whether overall levels of violent play or injuries were any greater in this period than in white rugby.

As with white rugby, women were not allowed to play rugby gener-ally, though as Emeran mentioned, some girls played rugby with boys when they were young. By puberty, women were excluded from the game and encouraged to play netball and hockey, though sports participation was much higher among non-Muslims.[41] Occasionally a woman's match formed part of the festivities at the annual charity Rag matches[42] in Cape Town, though it was not taken seriously by men. Despite this exclusion from playing, many women attended rugby matches and were strong supporters of the game. Matches involving leading teams, interprovincial play and Rag matches drew the community together. Men, women and children attended these matches together. As with rugby in other places, women provided domestic support. They also spent much time knitting scarves for players and supporters and made the special uniforms and scarves for Caledonian Roses and Stars for the Rag matches each year. The general attitude of Muslim men towards female participation in sport is evidenced in an interview with an Islamic woman who attended Trafalgar High School in District Six in the 1940s. She stated:

> I enjoyed PE because I could have a break from the classroom. I was not very good. But my other problem was that as a female coming from an Islamic background my father was not too pleased about me wearing a short skirt for classes. He allowed it [only] for school hours. This meant I could not play sport after school.[43].

Other than the famous Carnival that takes place every New Year, the Charity Rag match between Young Stars and Caledonian Roses became the focal point of annual community cultural celebration in Cape Town. Charity Rag began in 1936 as the two clubs adopted the annual fixture based on the model from the match played each year between the Universities of Cape Town and Stellenbosch. Notable features of the day were the four rugby matches played between the four teams from each club, colourful scarves knitted by women supporters of the clubs, songs composed for the occasion and the massive crowds of spectators at the Green Point Track. Ten thousand or more people from the Bo-Kaap and District Six used to walk down for the matches and processions from the District through the Bo-Kaap and down to the Track featured prominently.

Rag matches along with other elements of Coloured culture in Cape Town are evidence of a distinctive group culture that drew upon some aspects of white culture, but recast them into forms that fitted the realities of life in District Six and the Bo-Kaap. As with the Carnival, Rag provided a sense of cultural release, an event for community focus and solidarity and one where the wider system of segregation, racism and oppression could be forgotten for at least a short period of time. Rag and Carnival were celebrations of the community's vibrant culture and its resilience in the face of wider social, economic and political domination by whites. While local black sport was largely sustainable through its community links, national organisation of black sport was difficult and the creation of broadly inclusive associations within a wider racially seg-regated society was even harder to achieve.

National black rugby organisation and segregated sport

Black sport at the national level began to develop rapidly in the 1890s and early 1900s as local and regional associations appeared in Cape Town, Kimberley, Port Elizabeth and East London and soon after in Johannesburg and Durban. Many early national organisations were formed in Kimberley such as the SACRFB. This association included African and Coloured players and organised black rugby throughout the country, though the bulk of players were located in the urban centres of the Cape. Although some Africans initially were part of the SACRFB, by the early years of the twentieth century the majority of affiliated unions and players were Coloured. With its base in Kimberley, the SACRFB was located far from other centres of Coloured rugby in Cape Town, the Boland area and Port Elizabeth. The union did not have the finances nec-essary to run an effective national organisation on the level that could be mustered by the SARB in white rugby. Despite this, the association sur-vived due to the efforts of hard-working administrators who donated their time to the cause of rugby development. In order to improve the state of black sport, however, greater unity between sporting groups was needed from the national level downwards.

In the 1950s attempts began in many sports to unify blacks who had been divided into racially based associations. Three possibilities for sporting development emerged by the end of the decade. Black associa-tions could either merge into non-racial organisations, affiliate to white associations which began to encourage black associations to join them, though on a racially segregated basis, or maintain the status quo. The first two options held out the greatest advantages. Broad organisation of black sport would help challenge segregated sport and provide stronger competition. Affiliation with white organisations offered access to better facilities and funding though not equality. By the 1960s these issues came to a head as non-racial sporting bodies such as the South African Sports Association (SASA) and the South African Non-Racial Olympic

Committee (SANROC) appeared to challenge apartheid sport both internally and internationally.

Amalgamation of associations posed particular problems, however. Sporting organisations provided one of the few legitimate opportunities for blacks to be administrators and leaders, thus many officials tenaciously held on to their positions in sports administration. In the case of Coloured rugby, a personality clash developed between SACRFB leaders Abdullah Abass and Cuthbert Loriston as negotiations emerged between the SARB and the Coloured association for affiliation in the 1960s. The SARB president Danie Craven was keen to have Coloured rugby under the aegis of the SARB in order to fend off challenges to apartheid sport that were beginning to appear from overseas. Additionally, Craven had been involved in Coloured rugby, though unofficially, through coaching clinics for Coloured teams in the 1940s. Craven felt a close connection with many people in the Muslim community, some of whom were strong supporters of the Springbok rugby team when they played at Newlands in Cape Town. Coloured officials could not agree on the course of action to be taken, however, and this resulted in Loriston leading the majority of rural and small town clubs in the Boland region of the Western Cape into affiliation with the SARB as the South African Rugby Football Federation (SARFF) and those opposed to affiliation forming the SARU. The men who founded SARU demanded that any unified structure would have to be formed on the basis of merit selection for all representative rugby teams. Craven was unwilling to proactively desegregate rugby when all other South African sports remained segregated and the government encouraged the maintenance of racial segregation in sport. While talks for overall rugby unity were held periodically during the 1970s and 1980s, SARU took an increasingly hard line and followed the 1970s dictate of the non-racial sports movement that there should be no normal sport in an abnormal society. The SARU organised the bulk of non-racial rugby while the SARFF and an African association played in the racially segregated structures of the SARB.

As modern sports developed among blacks in South Africa, black sports people hoped to achieve recognition and opportunities available to white sports people, but as blacks became more successful, whites eliminated opportunities. This was particularly hard for sports people in cricket, rugby, netball, tennis and golf as mostly well-educated blacks played these sports, which were viewed as elements of 'civilised' culture. As a result, blacks were left with white standards as the norm for national teams, and top players were frequently compared with white stars to see if they 'would have made the grade'.[44] Due to better facilities, media coverage, opportunities to play and international competition, white elite sports remained the standard in the post-apartheid era. Much internal protest against apartheid in sport centred on the quite un-radical notion of equal opportunity through selection based on merit rather than on fundamental structural changes to a system that advantaged whites at the expense of other groups in the funding of sport and in access to quality facilities. Attitudes hardened in the 1970s and 1980s, as we discuss later, but the fundamental principle of merit selection survived in the post-apartheid period which has, perhaps ironically, helped to entrench the old sporting structures, though now unified with non-racial sporting organisations, in the new South Africa. We will return to this discussion in the last three chapters of the book.

Notes

1 For discussion of the literature on black sport, see J. Nauright, *Sport, Cultures and Identities in South Africa* (London, Leicester University Press, 1997 and Cape Town, David Phillip, 1997).
2 *Cape Times*, 26 October 1994.
3 A. Odendaal, '"The thing that is not round": the untold history of black rugby in South Africa', in A. Grundlingh, A. Odendaal and B. Spies, *Beyond the Tryline: Rugby and South African Society* (Johannesburg, Ravan, 1995), pp. 24–5.
4 B. Stoddart, 'Sport, cultural imperialism, and colonial response in the British Empire', *Comparative Studies in Society and History*, 30:4 (1988), p. 662.
5 District Six fell victim to the grand strategies of seperation of the races under the aegis of the Group Areas Act in apartheid South Africa. It was declared in 1966 by the government to be a residential area for whites. Despite opposition from the Cape Town city council, the area was razed and its more than 40,000 residents relocated between 1966 and 1971 to the Cape Flats area on the opposite side of Table Mountain. A technical college was built on the land, but very few whites ever moved into the area renamed Zonnebloem creating a substantial vacant area right next to the central business district of Cape Town. The area has been renamed District Six though arguments over future development were not settled in late 1997.
6 Gassan Emeran, interviewed by John Nauright, Cape Town, January 1995.
7 'Meneer' Effendi, interviewed by John Nauright, Cape Town, December 1994.
8 Odendaal, '"The thing that is not round"', p. 25.
9 Odendaal, '"The thing that is not round"', p. 33.
10 A. Odendaal, 'South Africa's black Victorians', in J. A. Mangan (ed.), *Pleasure, Profit, Proselytism: British Culture and Sport at Home and Abroad 1700–1914* (London, Frank Cass, 1988).
11 J. Iliffe, *A History of Modern Tanganyika* (Cambridge, Cambridge University Press, 1979).
12 O. Stuart, 'Players, workers, protesters: social change and soccer in colonial

Zimbabwe', in J. MacClancy (ed.), *Sport, Identity and Ethnicity* (London, Berg, 1996), p. 177.

13 T. Couzens, '"Moralising leisure time": the transatlantic connection and leisure activities on the Witwatersrand 1918–1930', in S. Marks and R. Rathbone (eds), *Industrialisation and Social Change in South Africa 1870–1930* (London, Longman, 1982).

14 A. Cobley, 'A political history of playing fields: the provision of sporting facilities for Africans in the Johannesburg area to 1948', *International Journal of the History of Sport*, 11:2 (1994), pp. 212–30.

15 For this discussion, see B. Willan, *Sol Plaatje: South African Nationalist 1876–1932* (Berkeley, University of California Press, 1984).

16 A. Odendaal, *Vukani Bantu! The Beginnings of Black Protest Politics in South Africa to 1912* (Cape Town, David Phillip, 1984), p. 62.

17 Odendaal, *Vukani Bantu*, p. 62.

18 Willan, *Sol Plaatje*, p. 247.

19 Stoddart, 'Sport, cultural imperialism, and colonial response', pp. 650–1.

20 B. Willan, 'An African in Kimberley', in S. Marks and R. Rathbone (eds), *Industrialisation and Social Change in South Africa 1870–1930* (London, Longman, 1982), p. 252.

21 R. Archer and A. Bouillon, *The South African Game: Sport and Racism* (London, Zed Press, 1982), pp. 115–16.

22 D. Pinnock, *The Brotherhoods: Street Gangs and State Control in Cape Town* (Cape Town, David Phillip, 1984), pp. 21–3.

23 Pinnock, *The Brotherhoods*.

24 Emeran interview.

25 For a preliminary discussion of muscular Islam in this context, see J. Nauright, 'Muscular Islam and Coloured Rugby in Cape Town, South Africa', *International Journal of the History of Sport*, 14:1 (1997), pp. 184–90.

26 The first records of Muslims playing officially in the CSRU that we have found date from 1961. Minute Books of the Perseverance Rugby Football Club, 1961. Thanks to Mark Wilson for providing access to these minute books.

27 Minute Books of the City and Suburban Rugby Union, 1931. Thanks to Herman Abrahams for providing access to these minute books.

28 Emeran interview. The notion of rugby as a 'second religion' has been most commonly applied to Afrikaners as discussed in the next chapter.

29 Effendi interview.

30 Emeran interview.

31 Effendi interview.

32 In the Cape, Coloureds had many voting and representative rights that did not extend to blacks in other areas of South Africa.

33 Pinnock, *The Brotherhoods*, p. 26.

34 *Skollies* referred to street youths who committed petty crimes. It is thought to be derived from a Dutch word meaning 'scavenger'.

35 Pinncok, *The Brotherhoods*, p. 26.

36 Pinnock, *The Brotherhoods*, p. 28.

37 Rajab Benjamin interviewed by John Nauright, Cape Town, December 1994.

38 Benjamin interview.

39 R. Rive, *Buckingham Palace, District Six* (London, Heinemann, 1986).

40 Benjamin interview.

41 Softball also attracted a number of Coloured women players by the 1950s and

remains popular amongst Coloured women.

42 Charity Rag, a key cultural event in the Coloured communities of the Bo-Kaap and District Six, began in 1936. Two clubs, the Young Stars and the Caledonian Roses, from the Bo-Kaap and District Six respectively, organised a charity match in aid of the hospital fund launched by the mayor of Cape Town. This match became an annual event, played every year except 1959, and its organisation reveals much about the cultural life of Coloureds in Cape Town.

43 Denise Jones interview, 1995.

44 Effendi interview.

Chapter 4

At the nexus of power:
rugby, the Broederbond and
the National Party during apartheid

As we have outlined in the previous two chapters, sport developed a significant following among white and black South Africans by the early
years of the twentieth century. As segregationist policies became more
entrenched during the 1920s and 1930s, however, it became increasingly
clear that their would be no cultural mixing based on education, adher-
ence to 'civilised' practices or class lines. As a result, cultural activities
were nearly completely separated and became politically charged. The
centrality of sport and sporting success in white South African society
and culture during the segregation and apartheid eras has received
much attention and discussion.[1] Recognition of the salience and sensitivity of sport during the apartheid period (1948–90) energised the diverse
sport boycott movement, especially from the mid-1960s, and prompted
widespread commentary from both activists and scholars.[2] Partly due to
mounting external pressure, sport came in for increasing attention at the
highest reaches of political power in apartheid South Africa, engaging
the attention of the closely interlinked Broederbond and the NP government. What has sometimes received less attention than it should,
however, is the important distinctions between the cultural and political
significance of different sporting codes and practices. It is impossible to
understand either the impact of the sport boycott or the policy responses
of South Africa's power elite without recognising these distinctions, and
the particular role played by rugby.[3]

Because of its extraordinary cultural and symbolic significance for
Afrikaners, rugby played a unique role in the calculations of the political
elite concentrated in the Broederbond and the NP. There was a high level
of interpenetration between the leadership of rugby and these organisations, as well as an active effort to gain control of rugby by them. There
were clear differences in the treatment of rugby and other sporting codes,
even very popular ones, as external and internal pressure on South
African sport grew. And, in response to these pressures, rugby can be

said, paradoxically, to have both led and trailed the process of change in South African sport policy and practice. In other words, it played a contradictory vanguard/rearguard role in the struggle for change in South African sport. In this chapter, we will explore each of these themes in turn.

The interpenetration of rugby, the Broederbond and the National Party

In order to situate and understand the place of rugby in relation to the nexus of power in the apartheid era, it is necessary to recall the sport's vital role in the construction of Afrikaner nationalism. Simply put, no other sporting practice – indeed no other cultural pursuit – became so closely tied up with Afrikaner identity in this extraordinary period than did rugby. As we discussed briefly in chapter 2, rugby progressively Afrikanerised during the 1930s and 1940s, culminating in the Broederbond attempting to control the administrative structures of the old imperial game at national and provincial levels.

The reasons and bases for this Afrikanerisation process have come in for increased scholarly attention. Albert Grundlingh emphasises the importance of institutional and social factors. In particular, he stresses the role of the University of Stellenbosch (comparable to the Oxford or Harvard of Afrikanerdom) in instilling a love of, and devotion to, the game among the pride of Afrikaner young men, and then sending its graduates out to proselytise for it from their socially privileged positions as church predikants and teachers.[4] Various authors have noted the importance of the symbolic meanings by which Afrikaners came to explain their special affinity for rugby – for example, its site on the border between civilisation and barbarism; its elitist connotations; its emphasis on group cohesion and the need to establish collective dominance over an opponent.[5] These values and associations helped to both construct and reinforce the ideological content of Afrikanerdom. Finally, rugby's association with Afrikaner nationalism was greatly facilitated by the success of Afrikaner players in South African rugby, and the success in turn of the Springbok national side. As *the* dominant international rugby power, only challenged by New Zealand, through the first half of the twentieth century, South Africa's rugby success came to symbolise both the actual and potential achievements of the Afrikaner people on a world scale (however limited the world of rugby, dominated by the old Commonwealth, was in practice[6]).

Rugby also enabled Afrikaners to indulge their continued animus towards the sons of the British Empire, both within South Africa and in international tests. Along with international success against British teams, a special intensity continued to attend matches between the Afrikaner and English medium universities and schools.[7] Moreover, the cherished Springbok symbol became the highest honour to which a young (especially male) white South African could aspire.[8] For any Canadian hockey, Norwegian skiing, or Cuban baseball devotee, this dynamic is not hard to comprehend. It is the stuff of which heroes – local, regional and national – are made.[9]

Under the circumstances, it was entirely natural that some successful rugby players would use the stature associated with sporting success as a springboard to subsequent positions of social, economic and political leadership. To cite just one conspicuous example, the former Springbok captain Dawid de Villiers, both a Broeder and a National Party member, used fellow Springboks in his campaign for the Johannesburg West constituency in 1972 (apparently to the consternation of his former mentor, SARB President Danie Craven[10]). De Villiers went on to hold a number of leading positions in the Cabinet, up to and including Minister of Environment in the post-apartheid Government of National Unity (GNU) until the NP's withdrawal from it in 1996. Leading Broeder and ex-Springbok Kobus Louw also had a long political career in the upper echelons of the NP. One could readily point to similar examples of some leading athletes becoming successful politicians in many countries.

Similarly, it is not surprising that leading rugby players and officials should be recruited into the Broederbond. The Broederbond was formed in 1918 as a secret (or confidential) organisation of male Afrikaners 'who strove for the ideal of an everlasting and separate Afrikaner nation . . . Its stated aim was the creation of a consciousness among Afrikaners concerning their language, religion, traditions, country, and volk, and the promotion of the interests of the Afrikaner nation'.[11] With closely interlocking memberships, the Broederbond and the NP together played a crucial role in mobilising and raising the consciousness of Afrikaners in the run-up to the NP's fateful electoral victory in 1948, and subsequently in devising and elaborating the policies of apartheid. As Hermann Giliomee explains, the Broederbond was not 'the secret body which rules South Africa',[12] as it was widely portrayed. Rather, its influence was more subtle, though still profound. It served as a crucial link between the NP and its Afrikaner ethnic constituency, helping to define policy alternatives, mobilise support for new policy initiatives, and 'take the pulse' of male Afrikanerdom. In this manner, it was a crucial element in the construction and maintenance of Afrikaner hegemony, understood in the Gramscian sense. Its influence waned only as class cleavages began to take hold and sow divisions within the Afrikaner elite itself.

Though rising to a membership of well over 10,000, the Broederbond remained an elite organisation, recruiting leading educators, churchmen, businessmen, bankers, lawyers and senior public servants, among others. Above all, it incorporated virtually all of the leading figures in the NP: in 1972, for example, its membership included the Prime Minister, virtually the entire Cabinet, and three-quarters of the members of the NP parliamentary caucus.[13] Members of the Broederbond executive were routinely also Cabinet Ministers, though not Prime Minister. Together, then, the NP and the Broederbond truly formed a nexus of elite political power in apartheid South Africa. It was into this nexus that many leading rugby players and officials were drawn.

There was both a natural and a deliberate element to this process. More naturally, it is not surprising that, in seeking to recruit the 'opinion leaders' of Afrikaner society, the Broederbond would look towards leading athletes and sports officials in general, and rugby players and officials in particular. After all, most Broeders, as good Afrikaner males, were also avid rugby enthusiasts. More deliberately, however, as awareness of the socio-political salience of sport grew, the Broederbond also took steps to put its own people in positions of authority in the rugby establishment. At the start of the apartheid era, control of the game was still largely in English-speaking white South African hands. Thereafter, Afrikaners principally associated with the Broederbond undertook a sustained campaign to wrest control for their own. Grundlingh reports that in the Transvaal it took at least twenty years for the process to be completed, with the 1965 campaign to put Broeder Jannie Le Roux in the presidency being 'carefully orchestrated and meticulously planned'.[14] In other areas and aspects of the game, however, success came more quickly. Many captains of the Springboks in the 1950s and 1960s were NP members or members of both the NP and the Broederbond. The captaincy of the Springbok side became an important symbolic prize for the Broeders, and following a sharp controversy over the selection of Basil Kenyon, an English-speaker, to lead the 1951 tour of the British Isles, Broeders within rugby brought pressure to bear to overturn the selection of Tommy Bedford as captain of a subsequent side in the late 1960s, and then to have the anti-government Bedford dropped from the side altogether.[15] Thereafter, with few exceptions (most notably the exceptionally talented Morné du Plessis, who subsequently played an influential role as manager of the side which won the 1995 Rugby World Cup), Springbok captains were either NP members, Broeders, or both.

At the level of rugby governance, the Broederbond also gained a high level of control. While Danie Craven, the legendary president of the SARB from 1956 until his death in 1993, was not a Broeder, all of his vice-presidents after 1959 were. Similarly, with the exception of one short tour in 1965, all managers of touring Springbok sides until the mid-1990s were Broederbond members.[16] Broederbond influence in rugby administration thus became pervasive, if not comprehensive. To give just one illustration of the way this nexus of power manifested itself, Broeder Kobus Louw was at one stage Secretary of the Department of Coloured Affairs and later a Cabinet Minister; in rugby he was vice-president of the SARB and manager of the 1965 tour to New Zealand.[17]

Beginning in the early 1970s, as South Africa's sports isolation grew and the country's political elite began to appreciate the implications of this process for its wider effort to maintain apartheid policies, the Broederbond launched a concerted campaign to place 'well disposed' people in control of sports organisations throughout South Africa. As the 1972 administrative report of the Broederbond's central executive body, the *Bondsraad*, put it:

> The fact that control of most sports is still in non-Afrikaner hands has resulted in our not being able to have a positive influence in all places. The Executive once again wants to appeal to Broeders to exert themselves to place well-disposed Afrikaners in control of sport. Sport exerts an important influence on competitors . . . and it is our duty in this way to eliminate wrong influences on young Afrikaner competitors.[18]

This campaign achieved a measure of success. However, by the time it was initiated, the process it sought to promote had been virtually completed in rugby.

The SARB President Danie Craven remained an important anomaly, however, which requires explanation. Why did the Broederbond never manage – or even, with limited exceptions, attempt – to replace him with one of their own? Grundlingh rightly points to Craven's forceful personality and wide-ranging overseas contacts. These strengths, combined with his eventual status as a virtual folk hero, meant that only a very formidable candidate indeed could be proposed to take his place. Moreover, 'It seems . . . that in broad ideological terms, the Broederbond was able to live with Craven'.[19] Indeed, it can be argued that, notwithstanding his professed hostility towards the Broederbond, Craven's own rather straightforward ideological outlook served the interests of the Afrikaner political elite very well.

Craven's most recent biographer, Paul Dobson, implies that there was Broederbond involvement in his election as President of the SARB in 1956, and that he was envisioned as what they termed a *skakel* – 'a non-Broeder put into an important position where the Broeders decided to exert influence. If he was a success, he would be manipulated. If he failed, there was no damage to a Broeder.'[20] Craven himself is described as anti-Broeder, doubtless in part because he resented their efforts to exercise such extensive control over himself and the game he loved. At one level, Craven proved much more independent-minded than the Nationalist elite would have hoped, and on at least a couple of occasions he broke spectacularly with government policy. The first was in sharply opposing Prime Minister Verwoerd's 1965 pronouncement that no Maoris would be allowed on All Black touring sides to South Africa. The second was in meeting with senior officials of the ANC in 1988 in Harare while the ANC was still a banned organisation, making the SARB the first major establishment sports body to do so.

Nevertheless, notwithstanding these stormy controversies (both of which proved to be relatively short-lived), Craven's leadership of rugby generally served the interests of the regime well. According to Dobson, his two-part 'non-negotiable principle' was 'that rugby's good and South Africa's good must be paramount'.[21] Otherwise, he is described as being politically naive – a view corroborated by Donald Woods.[22] Craven's straightforward patriotism to South Africa was largely unconditional, and was given to the Nationalists' South Africa just as readily as it would most probably have been given to the ANC's South Africa. The only time it brought him into conflict with the government was when they jeopardised his other core principle: devotion to the good of rugby.

For Craven, the good of South African rugby meant, first and foremost, the maintenance of international contacts and tours. He regarded the SARB's retention of its membership in the IRB as his greatest achievement as President,[23] and he worked assiduously to maintain overseas touring opportunities, and thus to break the international sports boycott. This eventually led him to organise several tours featuring some historically obscure international rivals, including South American and South Pacific opponents during the 1980s. Nevertheless, while touring opportunities narrowed inexorably, even to the exclusion of the passionate rivalry with the All Blacks after the tumultuous 1981 'Demo Tour',[24] there is little doubt that Craven was better positioned to promote continued international contacts than was any other South African. This was owing to his long and close associations with leading figures in the IRB and other rugby nations. It was in this regard that Craven's own personal code was precisely aligned with the interests of the NP and the Broederbond.

It bears emphasis that the nexus between rugby and the Afrikaner political elite served to strongly reinforce the masculine character of the latter. White South African society was, and generally remains, deeply patriarchal. Male hegemony was reflected in the composition of the parliamentary caucus and the Cabinet, and the privileged role played by the exclusively male Broederbond. But it was also strongly reinforced by the cultural centrality of rugby. This sport has been explored by Nauright and Chandler and their collaborators as a crucial vehicle for 'making men' where it has been popular.[25] Nowhere is this description more applicable than in South Africa. As a vital symbol of Afrikanerdom and a source of high status in Afrikaner society, rugby reinforced its essential masculinity.

Rugby in the South African sporting universe

Along with other formerly British settler societies in the southern hemisphere, white South Africa frequently has been described as 'sports mad'.[26] The extent and variety of sports participation and enthusiasm is extraordinarily high. Yet, as we noted at the outset, and notwithstanding the sporting accomplishments of South African athletes in a variety of endeavours, in order to understand the historical politics of South African sport, it is vitally important to distinguish the various meanings and identities attached to different sports. In particular, the distinctive place of rugby in the South African sporting universe must be understood. In this respect, Archer and Bouillon's label, 'the Chosen Sport of a Chosen People', is not far off the mark.[27] It is not that other sports were unimportant in South African sporting politics; rather, it is the way they related to and interacted with rugby which was historically so significant.

In the first place, the particular importance which the Afrikaner elite attached to rugby is reflected in the fact, noted above, that their efforts to gain control of rugby administration long predated those in other sporting codes – and remained most successful in the former. Indeed, it was largely the continuing pervasiveness of Afrikaner influence in the leadership of rugby, as well as its close identification with Afrikanerdom, which so bedevilled its adaptation to the new norms and expectations emerging in post-1990 South Africa.

The distinctive role and significance of rugby to the Afrikaner elite is also clearly indicated by their different reactions to isolation in various sporting contexts. The first major step in the isolation of South African sport occurred in 1964, with the suspension of South Africa from the International Olympic Committee (IOC) and its exclusion from the 1964 Tokyo Games.[28] An outsider might think that, given the world-wide profile of the Olympic Games, this would have been cause for grave concern among South Africa's political leaders, but government officials remained uncompromising and defiant in the face of South Africa's suspension.[29] From the perspective of the Afrikaner elite, IOC decision-making could be rationalised through the prism of its deeply anti-Communist ideological world-view, by virtue of the coalition of Third World and Eastern Bloc countries which had engineered its suspension. These were forces with which it would not compromise, even for the sake of Olympic sport.

This was followed, in 1965, by Prime Minister Hendrik Verwoerd's unanticipated announcement towards the end of a highly successful Springbok rugby tour of New Zealand that, consistent with apartheid policies, future All Black touring sides in South Africa would have to adhere to the traditional practice of excluding Maori players. The upshot was the cancellation of the planned 1967 All Black tour of South Africa. While Verwoerd's announcement did not have a discernible effect on the subsequent 1966 whites-only election, its consequence was clearly regarded as a different order of problem by NP decision-makers. It was principally the threatened loss of future rugby tours by traditional rivals, chief among them New Zealand, which prompted Verwoerd's successor as Prime Minister, John Vorster, to announce a shift in international sporting policy in April 1967. In future, 'he would not prescribe to any country with which South Africa had traditional ties on the composition of any team invited to South Africa'.[30] In the same speech, Vorster also announced South Africa's acceptance of the IOC requirement that only one team from each country would be permitted to participate in the Olympics, reversing the government's earlier insistence that white and black South Africans could only participate on separate teams. He obviously hoped that this would pave the way for South Africa's re-entry into the Olympics (it did not). Nevertheless, there can be little doubt that the principle impetus for this first significant sport policy shift was the desire to maintain rugby links with New Zealand and other traditional rivals –

a goal it was successful in achieving, at least in the short term. An All Black side incorporating three Maoris and one Samoan did tour South Africa in 1970.

Further evidence of the special place of rugby in the thinking of Afrikaner political leaders came not long after the reforms of 1967 with the celebrated d'Oliveira Affair. Basil d'Oliveira was a talented Coloured South African cricketer who had left for England in 1960 to pursue his playing career. Selected to replace an injured member of the MCC (English) side due to tour South Africa in late 1968, d'Oliveira's inclusion was regarded by Vorster as a deliberate provocation. He defiantly announced to cheering supporters at the Orange Free State NP Congress that a team including d'Oliveira would not be allowed to tour.[31] Admittedly, the affair was complicated by the fact that d'Oliveira was a South African, confounding the clear-cut distinction between domestic and international sport on which Vorster's 1967 reforms rested.[32] Nevertheless, his stance on this issue surely contradicted the essence of those reforms. To explain this contradiction, one needs to take account of the different identities and constituencies of the two sports. As Grundlingh argues, 'Narrow ethnic considerations seem to have been a factor in permitting concessions for rugby, but not for cricket'.[33] As discussed in chapter 2, cricket, though popular in white South Africa, was widely regarded as an English sport and did not hold anything like the interest and importance among Afrikaners that rugby did.[34] It could, therefore, be safely sacrificed by a Prime Minister anxious to balance the quest to maintain crucial international sporting links against the need to shore up government support among conservatives in his Afrikaner constituency. Ironically, Guelke argues compellingly that ultimately, the d'Oliveira Affair 'did most to bring about South Africa's isolation in international sport'.[35] At the time, however, this potential was either not appreciated or considered a price worth paying. Rugby links, by contrast, demanded a different kind of response.

South Africa's sporting isolation grew rapidly in the years that followed. In Britain, the Stop the Seventy Tour Campaign, organised under the leadership of the young South African Peter Hain primarily to force the cancellation of a planned Springbok cricket tour of England in 1970, successfully dogged the 1969 Springbok rugby tour with large-scale demonstrations and creative tactics. Its efforts were crowned with success when the 1970 cricket tour was cancelled.[36] Thereafter South Africa's isolation from test cricket became virtually complete, with only periodic 'rebel' tours to slake the thirst of South African players and fans for international competition. But more disturbing and disorienting to the Afrikaner political elite was the mounting international resistance to, and isolation in, test rugby. Aside from the protests against the 1969 tour of the British Isles, there were even larger demonstrations against the 1971 tour of Australia (the last to that country during the apartheid era), and above all the traumatic demonstrations marking the 1981 tour to New Zealand – the first to be televised in South Africa, and the last official test series in that cherished rivalry prior to 1992.[37] The latter is discussed in detail in the next chapter. Whereas isolation in virtually all other sports was ultimately expendable, this trend in rugby – a sport which, besides holding special salience for Afrikaner nationalists, was dominated internationally by the white, Western nations that apartheid South Africa considered its closest allies – had disturbing domestic implications, and prompted a telling policy response.

Finally, the distinctive importance of rugby was reflected in its leading role in the drama of splits within the Afrikaner political elite itself. First and most directly, it was Vorster's 1967 policy shift to allow Maoris in future touring sides from New Zealand that precipitated the departure of a group of *verkrampte* (conservative) Nationalists from the NP and the formation of the Herstigte (Restored) Nasionale Party (HNP) in 1969. At the September 1969 Transvaal Nationalist Party Congress former Cabinet Minister Albert Hertzog spoke out against the government's break with Verwoerd's policy of banning Maori All Blacks. As recounted by Guelke, 'He warned that the admission of Maoris would lead to social integration with Maoris dancing with Afrikaans girls on social occasions during the tour'.[38] Thereafter he and others who had voted against the government position on this issue were expelled from the party. The government then called an early election before the HNP was able to organise effectively, wiping out their parliamentary representation in the 1970 contest. Tactically, the government had turned back this right-wing challenge brilliantly, and the HNP never subsequently mounted a serious electoral challenge. Nevertheless, the split was indicative of the emerging struggles within the Afrikaner political elite over how best to maintain its hegemonic position, and how uncompromisingly to cling to Verwoerd's apartheid vision. The underlying issues were, of course, much bigger than the rugby controversy which brought them to a head; but it is nevertheless noteworthy that it was rugby which could trigger such deep feelings and divisions within the heretofore united Nationalist front.

Less directly, but still significantly, a rugby-based controversy also contributed to the much more serious split of 1982, when leading Broeder Dr Andries Treurnicht led fifteen MPs out of the NP caucus to form the Conservative Party. The primary cause of the split was the constitutional proposal of Vorster's successor, P. W. Botha, for a new Tricameral political system in which Coloured and Asian South Africans would be given the franchise and representation in separate parliamentary chambers. The Conservatives stood against the proposal and for 'racial preservation and the integrity of the *volk*'.[39] However, the final split was foreshadowed by a sharp controversy over the participation of a Coloured side in the 1980 Craven Week schools rugby tournament. Initiated in 1964 with high-minded aims of generating friendships, teaching sportsmanship and engendering a love of the game, Craven Week became a focal point for two areas of acute NP and Broederbond concern: rugby and education. In addition to becoming an intensely competitive event in which the top young talent of South African rugby would be assiduously scouted, Dobson writes that 'the week took on more and more the aspect of a Christian national youth festival, starting with a service in the Dutch Reformed Church, many exhortations, long grace before meals, a march-past to start it, and patriotic fervour.'[40]

In this highly charged atmosphere, heavily laden with Afrikaner nationalist symbolism and significance, it is not surprising that any steps toward racial mixing would generate resistance. Indeed, the controversy first surfaced two years before a SARFF team was included in Craven Week, when schoolmaster Jan Preuyt made a forceful closing address in which he announced that Craven Week would stay as it was – to the lusty cheers of his all-white audience. When Craven and the SARB insisted on the participation of a SARFF side in 1980, a storm of controversy ensued, with three East Rand schools refusing to send their boys for Craven Week trials. Craven himself then threatened that 'if schools boycotted Craven Week because of the participation of Coloureds, he would not allow their senior provincial teams to play'.[41] Craven's position in turn elicited sharp criticism from Treurnicht, who accused the SARB President of blackmail, breaking with his own party in so doing. This was, according to Dobson, 'Treurnicht's first big public confrontation with the National Party and it occurred despite the fact that he was a cabinet minister at the time'.[42] It helped to set the stage for the dramatic political split in Afrikanerdom that soon followed.

In sum, rugby's special significance for the Afrikaner political elite, manifested through its interpenetration with the Broederbond and the NP and its symbolic importance as *the* sport of Afrikaners, gave it a special place in the universe of South African sports and sports politics. This was reflected in the pursuit by elite Afrikanerdom of administrative control and leadership of the game, their extreme sensitivity to and differential treatment of threats to its international links, and rugby's prominent role in some of the most important confrontations in elite Afrikaner politics. This special salience also meant that it played a leading, yet paradoxically resistant, role in the process of sports policy reform as it evolved from 1967 onwards.

Rugby's contradictory role in driving policy change

The first break in apartheid South Africa's strict segregationist sports policy came in 1967 when Prime Minister Vorster announced that, among other things, South Africa would now be prepared to host racially mixed touring sides from traditional friends. It was the threatened loss of rugby ties with New Zealand that was the direct cause of this policy shift – a shift which was, as we have seen, sufficiently controversial to precipitate the split in Afrikanerdom leading to the formation of the HNP. Thereafter the NP government, in close collaboration with the Broederbond, undertook a series of changes, or reforms, to sports policy. While it would be inaccurate to suggest that these reforms were driven exclusively by a desire to maintain rugby links, it can be argued that the Afrikaner elite's peculiar preoccupation with rugby was a vital influence in shaping their distinctly contradictory nature. More precisely, the intense desire of this elite's core Afrikaner constituency to have continued access to international rugby competition, and the political risks of losing those links, necessitated a response aimed at persuading the international sports community that South African sport was evolving in the direction of internationally accepted norms of open and integrated competition. On the other hand, the continued staunch resistance of a vocal, hard-line element within the rugby-loving Afrikaner community to domestic integration, especially in a contact sport like rugby, required a degree of ambiguity and contradiction in the reforms which largely vitiated their integrative implications.

If a claim that international rugby controversies directly *caused* specific changes in sports policy would be too strong, there was certainly a close correlation. After the 1967 reform, the next significant step was taken in 1971, when the government introduced a new multinational sports policy. Under the terms of this policy, international teams visiting South Africa were permitted to include matches against black teams and black

South African athletes were allowed to participate in open international competitions in South Africa, as long as they were members of sports bodies affiliated to white federations – i.e., *not* associated with non-racial bodies linked to SACOS (in the case of rugby, SARU). This new departure followed an extensive, carefully orchestrated process of consultation with both the leadership and subsequently the rank-and-file of the Broederbond, designed to keep this influential constituency onside through these risky changes and to use them to sell the shift to the wider Afrikaner electorate.[43] Temporally, it followed the d'Oliveira Affair, but more particularly the massive protests which greeted the rugby Springboks in the British Isles (1969) and Australia (1971). The new policy was carefully designed to allow South Africa to present itself to the world as permitting multiracial competition, while preserving the racialist multinational vision of grand apartheid at home. The contradiction was too transparent, however: the sporting world was not persuaded.

In 1976, therefore, multinationalism was extended downwards to the club level. Policy implementation, however, was marked by a high degree of incoherence and inconsistency, reflecting the government's wish to be seen to be simultaneously adhering to the requirements of racial separation and the promotion of Afrikaner identity at home, while moving 'intelligently toward a normalisation of [race] relations' in the eyes of the international community.[44] Temporally, the policy shift followed the widening of the scope of the sport boycott when twenty-one African nations and Guyana boycotted the 1976 Montreal Olympics in protest over the participation of New Zealand following its rugby tour of South Africa earlier that year – once again placing rugby at the epicentre of controversy.

The contradictions and limitations in this policy shift were well illustrated by the celebrated case of the Watson brothers, including Dan 'Cheeky' Watson, an Eastern Province winger who had been widely touted as a future Springbok. When the Watsons joined a SARU-affiliated club in the Port Elizabeth area in 1977, Cheeky and his brother Valance were arrested for being in an African township without a permit. Ultimately, the government decided not to pursue prosecution on the advice of Minister of Sport Piet Koornhof, who judged that this would generate too much adverse publicity internationally.[45] Subsequently, however, Cheeky Watson's home was fire-bombed, indicating the seriousness with which defections from white establishment rugby were viewed.

Finally, in the late 1970s and early 1980s, the government shifted policy again to one of autonomy for sport. It abolished the Department of Sport and Leisure in 1982, replacing it with a Directorate of Sport Advancement within the Department of National Education, and it amended apartheid legislation[46] so that it would no longer impinge on sporting events. 'In effect', according to a report of the Australian Department of Foreign Affairs, 'decisions about racial segregation were shifted from the Government to local authorities, private bodies, and individuals'.[47] These shifts followed the trauma of the 1981 Springbok tour of New Zealand, discussed in the next chapter.

The symbolic and socio-psychological implications of these changes were arguably of some real significance, notably in undermining the legitimacy of apartheid principles and policies. Yet as the Australian report implies, and numerous critics pointed out, the policy shifts failed to fundamentally alter the prevailing balance of opportunities in sport, embedded as it was in the racist and highly unequal social, political and economic structures of the country: hence the logic of the SACOS slogan, 'No normal sport in an abnormal society'. It made little difference to most black South Africans that they were legally *allowed* to participate in the activities of historically white clubs if they were unable to get to such clubs' remote training facilities, or indeed to achieve adequate performance levels due to limitations on coaching, facilities, nutrition, etc. during the formative stages of their athletic development in their own areas. Moreover, in the critical realm of school sports, the government rejected proposals which would have paved the way for increased integration by creating a single School Sports Council, insisting that school sport should be guided by the over-riding policy of treating education as an 'own [racial group] affair'. As John Davies noted in 1985, 'It is quite simply impossible for non-discriminatory sport to emerge from such a racially disfigured foundation' at the school level.[48]

Conclusion

The sports policy reforms on which rugby was arguably the single most important influence followed a distinctly contradictory pattern. On the one hand, they were motivated by a strong desire to persuade the rest of the sporting world – particularly the white, Western sporting world – that change towards integrated sport was well underway, and hence that South Africa should be 'rewarded' by the restoration of full international sporting links.[49] On the other hand, they were limited by the government's desire to reassure its more conservative followers – the most passionate of rugby supporters – that it was in no way opening the door to fully integrated sport at home. Thus, while it could be argued that rugby was the principal precipitator of sports reforms, it was also paradoxically perceived as the sporting code most resistant to *real* change. This contradictory role and image was to persist both immediately prior to and during the transitional period, beginning with the SARB's dramatic Harare summit with the ANC in 1988, as discussed in chapter 6. In the meantime, however, South Africa's international rugby links ultimately became the principle target for the transnational sports boycott movement, contributing significantly to the growth of external pressure for change. And of these links, the storied rivalry with the small antipodean state of New Zealand emerged as the most important battle ground.

Notes

1 For a detailed discussion of the role of sport during segregation, apartheid and into the post-apartheid era, see J. Nauright, *Sport, Cultures and Identities in South Africa* (London, Leicester University Press, 1997 and Cape Town, David Phillip, 1997).

2 See, for example, R. Archer and A. Bouillon, *The South African Game: Sport and Racism* (London, Zed Press, 1982); P. Hain, *Don't Play with Apartheid* (London, George Allen and Unwin, 1971); B. Kidd, 'The campaign against sport in South Africa', *International Journal*, 43:4 (1988), pp. 643–64; and A. Guelke, 'The politicisation of South African sport', in L. Allison (ed.), *The Politics of Sport* (Manchester, Manchester University Press, 1986), pp. 118–48.

3 For related arguments see A. Grundlingh, 'Playing for power: rugby, Afrikaner Nationalism and masculinity in South Africa', in J. Nauright and T. J. L. Chandler (eds), *Making Men: Rugby and Masculine Identity* (London, Frank Cass, 1996), pp. 181–204; Archer and Bouillon, *The South African Game*, pp. 294–301; and J. Nauright and D. Black, 'It's rugby that really matters: New Zealand–South Africa rugby relations and the moves to isolate South Africa, 1956–1992', in R. Wilcox (ed.), *Sport in the Global Village* (Morganstown, W. Va, Fitness Information Technology, 1994), pp. 165–83.

4 Grundlingh, 'Playing for power', pp. 106–11.

5 See, for example, Grundlingh, 'Playing for power', pp. 111–15; Archer and Bouillon, *The South African Game*, pp. 64–75; and D. Lewis, 'Soccer and rugby: popular production of pleasure in South African culture', *Southern African Political and Economic Monthly*, 6: 3–4 (1992/93), pp. 13–17.

6 Donald Woods suggests that the realisation that even most other rugby powers did not accord rugby its due national paramountcy dawned on Afrikaner South Africans only in the late 1960s. See Woods, *Black and White* (Dublin, Ward River Press, 1981), p. 49.

7 Woods recounts how, playing school rugby for his English-speaking school against Afrikaner opponents, 'It was as if they were fighting the Boer War all over again, with us cast in the role of "the English"', Woods, *Black and White*, p. 47.

8 See D. Booth, 'Mandela and *Amabokoboko*: the political and linguistic nation-alisation of South Africa?', *Journal of Modern African Studies*, 34:3 (1996), pp. 461–6.

9 For a compelling expression of rugby's role in the making of Afrikaner heroes, see Alan Paton's novel, *Too Late the Phalarope* (New York, Charles Scribner, 1953). On the role of 'national' sports, see M. Goksoyr, 'Our games – our virtues? "National Sports" as symbols: a discussion of idealtypes', in F. J. G. van der Merwe (ed.), *Sport as Symbol, Symbols in Sport* (Sankt Augustin, Academia, 1996), pp. 363–70.

10 P. Dobson, *Doc: The Life of Danie Craven* (Cape Town, Human and Rousseau, 1994), p. 135.

11 H. Giliomee, 'The National Party and the Afrikaner Broederbond', in R. Price and C. Rosberg (eds), *The Apartheid Regime* (Berkeley, Institute of International Studies, 1980), p. 38. See also J. H. P. Serfontein, *Brotherhood of Power* (London, Rex Collings, 1979), and I. Wilkins and H. Strydom, *The Broederbond* (New York and London, Paddington Press, 1979).

12 Giliomee, 'The National Party', p. 40.

13 Giliomee, 'The National Party', p. 39.

14 Grundlingh, 'Playing for power', pp. 121–2.

15 Woods, *Black and White*, p. 45.

16 Dobson, *Doc*, pp. 133–4.

17 Dobson, *Doc*, pp. 160–4.

18 Wilkins and Strydom, *The Broederbond*, p. 247.

19 Grundlingh, 'Playing for power', p. 122.

20 Dobson, *Doc*, p. 134.

21 Dobson, *Doc*, p. 255.

22 Woods, *Black and White*, pp. 45–6.

23 Dobson, *Doc*, p. 142.

24 The one partial exception to the severing of rugby links with New Zealand was the clandestinely organised 1986 rebel tour of the New Zealand Cavaliers, involving most of New Zealand's top players and regular All Blacks. It was organised by the then-President of the Transvaal Rugby Union and later President of the integrated SARFU, the ubiquitous Louis Luyt, ostensibly without Craven's knowledge. It also caused great consternation in IRB circles.

25 Nauright and Chandler (eds), *Making Men*; and Grundlingh, 'Playing for power', pp. 126–30.

26 See Archer and Bouillon, *The South African Game*, pp. 1–14.

27 Archer and Bouillon, *The South African Game*, pp. 56–78.

28 On these events, see S. Quick, '"Black Knight Checks White King": the conflict between Avery Brundage and the African Nations over South African Membership of the IOC', *Canadian Journal of History of Sport*, 21:2 (1990), pp. 20–4.

29 See R. Lapchick, *The Politics of Race and International Sport* (Westport, Conn., Greenwood, 1975), pp. 60–3.

30 Guelke, 'The politicisation of South African sport', p. 128. Verwoerd had been assassinated in September 1966.

31 See Guelke, 'The politicisation of South African sport', pp. 130–1; and Lapchick, *The Politics of Race and International Sport*, pp. 120–9.

32 Point made by Guelke, 'The politicisation of South African sport', p. 130.

33 Grundlingh, 'Playing for power', p. 125.
34 Donald Woods recounts how the Springbok cricket side about to set off for a tour of England in 1951 was introduced to Prime Minister D. F. Malan who, after several minutes of conversation, astonished his compatriots by saying, 'I hope you enjoy your visit to South Africa', Woods, *Black and White*, pp. 46–7.
35 Guelke, 'The politicisation of South African sport', p. 130.
36 See Hain, *Don't Play with Apartheid*.
37 See Nauright and Black, 'It's rugby that really matters'; and Archer and Bouillon, *The South African Game*, pp. 294–301.
38 Guelke, 'The politicisation of South African sport', pp. 129–30, citing Serfontein, *Brotherhood of Power*, p. 214. See also T. R. H. Davenport, *South Africa, a Modern History*, 2nd edition (Toronto, University of Toronto Press, 1978), pp. 305–7.
39 W. Beinart, *Twentieth-Century South Africa* (Oxford, Oxford University Press, 1994), pp. 230–1.
40 Dobson, *Doc*, pp. 209–10.
41 Dobson, *Doc*, p. 211.
42 Dobson, *Doc*, p. 211.
43 See Wilkins and Strydom, *The Broederbond*, pp. 239–52, and Serfontein, *Brotherhood of Power*, pp. 153–4. For good accounts of the reform process as a whole, see Guelke, 'The politicisation of South African sport', and W. Munro, 'The state and sports: political maneuvering in the civil order', in W. James (ed.), *The State of Apartheid* (Boulder, Lynne Rienner, 1987), pp. 117–42.
44 Munro, 'The state and sports', p. 129.
45 See Archer and Bouillon, *The South African Game*, p. 267; and Woods, *Black and White*, pp. 67–8.
46 Specifically, the Group Areas Act, the Liquor Act and the Black Urban Areas Consolidation Act.
47 Department of Foreign Affairs and Trade (Australia), 'Race and rugby in South Africa', *Australian Foreign Affairs Review*, 59:4 (1988), p. 141.
48 J. Davies, 'Politics, sport and education in South Africa', *African Affairs*, 86 (1985), p. 363.
49 Craven's SARB undertook extraordinary measures to reinforce this message. Most conspicuously, he organised the International Rugby Media Congress in August 1983, whereby fifty-five international rugby writers were invited to an expensive 'nothing-to-hide, face-the-facts attempt to win the world's media to his side', Dobson, *Doc*, p. 233.

Chapter 5
Springbok–All Black rugby, sanctions and politics, 1959–92[1]

While rugby became important for white men and white South African society in general, it was particularly crucial that the Springbok national rugby team do well against its rivals. International tours and matches became focal points of white cultural identity, and success increasingly took on political relevance as a way to shore up white insecurities and to demonstrate the symbolic power of white South Africa. In particular, matches against the British Lions were significant opportunities for Afrikaners to teach *die Engelse* a lesson. Donald Woods recounts how, in the course of the disastrous (for the Springboks) 1974 Lions tour of South Africa, as the losses mounted, team meetings became increasingly 'Afrikanerised . . . The national coach, Johan Claassen, a leading Broederbonder, eventually spoke no English at all in his team talk, and the burden of his message no longer had to do with tactics but with the patriotic duty of Afrikaners to strike a sacred blow for the Volk'.[2] Most important of all for Springbok supporters, however, were matches against arch-rivals for world supremacy, the New Zealand All Blacks. Ironically, until 1970 the All Black touring sides to South Africa were all white. South Africa only played full strength All Black sides before that time when they toured New Zealand, where Maoris were also on All Black teams. Because of the cultural and political significance of the Springbok–All Black relationship to the maintenance of traditional international cultural links, the anti-apartheid movement in sport spent much time trying to prevent and disrupt tours between South Africa and New Zealand. After 1970, when virtually every other major South African sport had been isolated from official international competition, rugby became a crucial battle ground. Both the South African government and the anti-apartheid movement focused on international rugby links as a cultural area where apartheid could be shored up or broken down in a psychological sense.

While acknowledging the role of sports sanctions in levering limited changes in sports policy and practice from the South African regime, many political analysts have been reticent about claiming broader political influence for them. Anthony Payne's assessment of the influence of the Commonwealth's Gleneagles Agreement on Apartheid and Sport is representative. Having noted the complex internal and external factors precipitating the changes unleashed in South Africa in early 1990, he argues that:

> In the circumstances, it is wise to be cautious: Gleneagles was part of a broader demonstration of external opposition to apartheid which unquestionably had an effect on the political outlook of the Afrikaner political elite. But, of itself, the abrogation of sporting contacts between the Commonwealth and South Africa cannot be reckoned to have counted for much and, certainly, some of the wilder claims made both on behalf of and against the boycott should be discounted.[3]

Without resorting to 'wild claims', we contend that a historically grounded understanding of the significance of rugby union football in South African and New Zealand societies allows a bolder, more precise assessment of the role of sport in general, and rugby in particular, in contributing to the dismantling of apartheid.[4]

Although all forms of international pressure on and isolation of South Africa had their supporters, sanctions advocates were overwhelmingly concerned with economic (trade and financial) measures.[5] This preoccupation was reflected, for example, in the 1989 report of a 'distinguished group of [sanctions] experts and researchers' to the Commonwealth Committee of Foreign Ministers on Southern Africa. *The Sanctions Report* argued that:

> After a detailed study of the available data we conclude that there is a threshold and that sanctions must be greater than that threshold if they are to have the required impact. *We believe that a sustained cut in South African imports of 30 per cent is the minimum that would produce a fall in GDP that was sufficient to trigger an appropriate political response* . . . [The report goes on] *to be politically effective, sanctions would need to cut world-wide purchases from South Africa by at least one quarter.*[6]

Yet within months of this argument, and without these figures being approached, the process of negotiation to dismantle apartheid had begun.

These experts, like many others, had discounted the importance of other sources of pressure for change or, perhaps more accurately, misunderstood the dynamics of this process. Pressures and incentives from several sources as well as the bold, opportunistic calculations of the NP government under F. W. de Klerk, all contributed to changes after 1989.[7] Internal resistance, in particular, became vital. But given the over-whelming power of the state's security apparatus and the high, if stagnant, standard of living enjoyed by most whites, neither the limited external economic sanctions pressure nor the domestic unrest of the 1980s were sufficiently strong to force the government's hand in 1989. Bluntly stated, most Afrikaners and other white South Africans simply did not manifest the stubborn determination to defend their apartheid-based way of life that most observers had anticipated. Their vaunted will to resist external and internal pressure was weaker than estimated, and their desire for reintegration into the international cultural and economic mainstream was stronger.

In the unexpectedly rapid erosion of white South Africa's will to resist exogenous pressure and the heightening of its longing to win reacceptance into the international community, the impact of sports sanctions in general, and rugby sanctions in particular, were important.[8] The significance of sport to white South Africans was demonstrated clearly by the government's use of it in the March 1992 whites-only referendum campaign on constitutional negotiations. South Africa's Cricket World Cup success and the impending return to international rugby were key elements in the government's arguments for a 'yes' vote.[9] Not insignificantly, Eddie Tonks, President of the New Zealand Rugby Football Union (NZRFU), was in South Africa immediately prior to the referendum vote to negotiate the dates for a New Zealand tour of South Africa for August 1992,[10] even though 1992 tour arrangements had been discussed previously.

The use of sport in the referendum campaign suggests that those who had long advocated South Africa's isolation from international sport were right in their assumptions concerning the potential effects of sport boycotts on white South Africa. As early as 1971, Peter Hain argued that as pressure increased the South African government and sporting officials would have to make concessions.[11] Despite those views, the weight of sports (especially rugby) sanctions in the years prior to the launching of the reform process was substantially over-looked by most sanctions analysts.

In order to understand the full political significance of rugby sanctions, it is necessary to briefly outline the historical role of international rugby success in the dominant cultures of both South Africa and New Zealand. In both countries, rugby has been a crucial element in the forging of national male, and mostly white, identities throughout the twentieth century. As such, its cultural and political significance has far exceeded that of 'just a game'.

Rugby and the construction of national identity in South Africa and New Zealand

South Africa and New Zealand shared historical experiences as white-dominated settler societies within the British Empire, within which close relations were reinforced through sporting and other cultural links. Early rugby tours of the British Isles were vital in forging emergent national identities at crucial junctures as we have seen in the 1906 Springbok tour of the British Isles.[12]

New Zealand sociologist and activist Richard Thompson summed up the passion for rugby in both South Africa and New Zealand in his 1975 book, *Retreat from Apartheid*. South Africa and New Zealand, he asserts, share 'not merely a passion for rugby, but a similar approach to the game, and the rugby rivalry is felt to be distinctive. . . . [T]o play it the hard way is to play it the man's way'. He continues, 'a defeat reflects unfavourably on the quality of New Zealand manhood and its way of life'.[13] The famous late South African author and former Liberal Party leader, Alan Paton, stated that 'white South Africans are madly enthusiastic about rugby, and *especially about playing New Zealand*'.[14] And Donald Woods, former South African newspaper editor and confidante of Steve Biko, recalls from his childhood that 'Springbok–All Black rugby was full of tradition and lore. For us it was the greatest of international rivalries, and during World War Two whenever South African and New Zealand troops encountered each other, whether in a Cairo street or a London pub, they would scrum down on the spot.'[15] In addition to these testimonials concerning the role of rugby in South Africa and New Zealand, it should be remembered that for much of this century the sport was compulsory for white boys in South African schools and the only winter sport offered in many New Zealand schools before the 1970s.[16] This has meant that most members of the dominant group in both societies shared a common cultural practice – rugby.

Several New Zealand authors have called rugby New Zealand's 'secular religion'. To become an All Black has represented a peak of social status transcending all other categories.[17] A delegate to a 1970 conference of the New Zealand Race Relations Council suggested the power of rugby within New Zealand society: 'What can you do when we have a Rugby Union that is even more influential than the Government?'[18]

Similarly, as discussed in chapter 4, rugby in apartheid South Africa has been described as 'the Afrikaner's second religion',[19] and 'the Afrikaner's *real* sport in South Africa', which 'comes close to a religious zeal, from school level upward'.[20]

Although officials in both countries attempted to down-play links between rugby and politics, it is clear that the two were closely intertwined from the early twentieth century. In 1905, New Zealand Prime Minister Richard Seddon was labelled 'Minister of Football' after the press revealed he had match reports from Britain cabled out as government messages.[21] In both countries many international and first-class rugby players have attained positions of power in government and business. In South Africa, as we have seen, there have been close links between Springbok captains, the ruling NP and the secret Afrikaner Broederbond, whose members controlled many positions of power in post-World War Two South African society.[22]

International rugby and mounting political controversy

Rugby relations between South Africa and New Zealand since the 1920s have been a persistent source of debate, especially in New Zealand. The origins of these debates are rooted in the two countries' differing experiences of race relations. New Zealand's general policy approach since the Treaty of Waitangi of 1840 attempted to include Maoris within a wider, albeit white-defined, society, while South African racial policies in the twentieth century were (until 1994) based on principles of racial segregation and white domination. In 1921 the Springboks played the Maori All Blacks (winning by a point). The emerging difference in racial attitudes was summed up after the match by a South African reporter named Blackett who was 'sickened' at the sight of white New Zealanders cheering for Maoris against members of their own race.[23] However, the best New Zealand rugby player of the 1920s, George Nepia, was excluded from selection for the 1928 All Black tour of South Africa because he was Maori.

Exclusion of Maoris from tours of South Africa sparked little controversy in New Zealand before World War Two. After the South African NP came to power in 1948 and set about implementing apartheid, however, sporting contacts began to be questioned by a handful of New Zealanders. This took several years to develop as there was no protest during the 1956 Springbok tour of New Zealand. It seemed as if the whole country united behind the single goal of defeating South Africa to avenge the humiliating test series whitewash of 1949. In those days before television and close links between New Zealand and the outside world, awareness of South Africa was largely confined to its status as a rugby power and an ally in the British Empire and in World War Two.[24]

When debate about rugby contacts developed in 1959, it centred on the exclusion of Maoris from trials for the proposed 1960 All Black tour of South Africa and the NZRFU's complicity with South African requests that they be excluded, rather than on the internal racial policies of the South African government. The slogan New Zealand protesters developed was 'No Maoris, no tour', and anti-tour petition drives were organised by the Citizens All Black Tour Association (CABTA) and by groups within South Africa including the SASA, recently formed to promote non-racial sport.[25] Thousands of South Africans and New Zealanders petitioned the New Zealand government to cancel the tour, with CABTA obtaining over 162,000 signatures out of a total New Zealand population of under three million. Still, Prime Minister Walter Nash decided not to interfere with the decision of the NZRFU on the tour, confirming his Labour Party's then policy of non-interference with sporting bodies.[26]

Protests in New Zealand increased sharply after the South African police massacred peaceful protesters at Sharpeville on 21 March 1960. In protest over the killings, the New Zealand Cargo Workers' Union passed a resolution strongly condemning the loss of life, and urged that the situation 'now makes it imperative that no New Zealand team at all should go to a country with such a black record of mass murder'.[27] Despite the growing domestic protests and emerging international opposition resulting from Sharpeville, the NZRFU went ahead with the 1960 tour.

From 1960 onwards, the South African government appreciated the threat protesters in New Zealand could pose to future rugby relations. In addition, after South Africa was barred from the Olympic Games in 1964 and 1968, and expelled from the Olympic movement in 1970, the continuation of international rugby tours became a crucial element in South Africa's international sports and broader diplomatic strategies. As discussed in chapter 4, both the ruling NP and the opposition United Party rationalised expulsion from the Olympics as part of a Moscow-orchestrated Communist onslaught. However, both parties viewed international rugby (and to a lesser degree, cricket) as an integral part of white South Africa's historical and cultural ties to European 'civilisation'.[28] As a result of these developments, New Zealand was targeted by the South African government on the one hand, and the international sports boycott movement and exiled South African non-racial sporting organisations on the other, as the key to making or breaking sports boycott strategies.

Prime Minister Hendrik Verwoerd, the architect of apartheid, chose to keep quiet during the run-up to the 1965 Springbok tour of New Zealand, refusing to comment on whether Maoris would be excluded from future tours to South Africa. But prior to the last international match in 1965, he announced that all future teams touring South Africa would have to abide by South Africa's local custom. It was clear to New Zealanders that this meant no Maoris. Prime Minister Keith Holyoake subsequently told parliament that New Zealand could not 'be fully and truly represented by a team chosen on racial lines'.[29] As a result, the NZRFU postponed the proposed All Black tour of 1967.

In 1966, Verwoerd was assassinated, and the less rigid John Vorster became Prime Minister. Rather than face the possibility of no further tours of South Africa by the All Blacks, in 1968 Vorster made a dramatic decision allowing the NZRFU to send Maoris on upcoming tours.[30] This step was the first real attempt by the South African government to alleviate international pressure in the sports arena, and heralded the myriad of reformist measures over the next twenty years discussed in the previous chapter. Consequently, in 1970, the NZRFU sent a team to South Africa that included three Maoris and one Samoan.

Protests against the 1970 tour in New Zealand, and against the proposed 1973 Springbok tour of New Zealand, were partly motivated by concerns that Christchurch might lose its bid to host the 1974 Commonwealth Games. These concerns arose, in part, out of New Zealand's record of support for South Africa in international organisations. New Zealand's record on UN resolutions against South Africa in the 1960s was regarded by non-white dominated Commonwealth states, among others, as distinctly unimpressive, as it voted against or abstained on nearly every resolution that condemned South Africa.[31] The New Zealand member also staunchly defended South Africa at the IOC meeting that expelled it from the Olympic movement in 1970. In addition, African Commonwealth leaders used Australia's new tough stance on sporting contacts with South Africa to pressure the New Zealand government to take a similar stand against competition with South Africa until racial discrimination in sport was abolished.[32]

In 1969, South Africa sent one of its most senior diplomats, P. H. Phillip, to New Zealand to serve as Consul-General. Phillip distributed much pro-government information on South Africa, wrote numerous newspaper columns, and spoke to countless groups during his tenure, which lasted until 1976. He also held numerous social functions to which many All Blacks and National Party MPs and Cabinet Ministers were invited. Commentators at the time pointed out that he was a very senior diplomat to be sent to such an unimportant country as New Zealand, with whom South Africa's economic (and strategic) relations were 'insignificant'.[33] Vorster's government, however, clearly thought the maintenance of rugby links with New Zealand was important both for white support at home, and from the standpoint of attempts to combat growing sanctions movements internationally. This highlights the thoroughly unorthodox character of South African diplomacy through the apartheid era.

Despite its expulsion from the Olympic movement in 1970 and banning from most other international sporting organisations in the 1960s and early 1970s, South Africa remained firmly entrenched on the IRB along with other white-dominated countries: New Zealand, Australia, England, Scotland, Ireland, Wales and France. To the government and many white South Africans, sporting isolation could be tolerated as long as rugby could still be played. Norman Middleton, President of the non-racial SACOS, stated in 1976:

> It has to be realized that to genuine Afrikaners – the NP is substantially Afrikaner from top to bottom – rugby of all sports has a mystical significance and importance. I don't think that the Government could care less about such sports as cricket and soccer. They don't really mean much to the true Afrikaner.
>
> Therefore the expulsion of the country from international competition in these sports doesn't mean too much. But RUGBY IS DIFFERENT. RUGBY IS THE AFRIKANER'S SECOND RELIGION.[34]

Springbok–All Black rugby again was threatened in 1973. A proposed tour of that year was cancelled by the newly elected New Zealand Labour government headed by Norman Kirk. Kirk's initial policy was one of non-interference, but he commissioned a police report on the possible levels of protest during a South African tour. The police report stated that more than 10,000 demonstrators could be mustered in the major cities of Auckland, Wellington and Christchurch if the Springboks toured, possibly engendering 'the greatest eruption of violence the country has ever known'.[35] This report, combined with threats from black Commonwealth countries to boycott the 1974 Commonwealth Games in Christchurch, eventually forced Kirk's hand. The NZRFU, for its part, left it to the Prime Minister to determine the fate of the tour, calculating that he (and not they) would be stigmatised by a decision to cancel. An attempt by the SARB to include token blacks in the tour party was exposed on the eve of the tour, and Kirk was finally forced to call it off. Subsequently, in 1974, he reversed Labour's historic position of non-intervention, stating that any team representing any sporting organisation which practised apartheid at any level would not be welcome in New Zealand.

Politically, the cancellation of the rugby tour proved damaging to the Labour government. The new, populist National Party leader, Robert Muldoon, made rugby relations with South Africa a campaign issue in the 1975 election, which the National party won easily.[36] Although the Springboks did not immediately come to New Zealand, the All Blacks toured South Africa in 1976. As international outrage mounted over the juxtaposition of the All Black tour with the Soweto student uprisings, twenty-one African countries plus Guyana boycotted the 1976 Montreal Olympics in protest against New Zealand's participation. This marked a significant extension of the broader sports boycott, as for the first time third-party countries or athletes that had competed in South Africa were targeted for sanctions.

In 1977, a Canadian effort to avoid a similar boycott of the 1978 Edmonton Commonwealth Games, again over New Zealand–South Africa rugby links, led to the adoption by Commonwealth Heads of Government of the Gleneagles Declaration on Apartheid and Sport. The Gleneagles Agreement called on all Commonwealth governments to discourage sporting contacts with South Africa.[37] Spearheaded by the Canadian government and orchestrated by the Commonwealth Secretariat, it subsequently emerged as perhaps the most important international landmark in extending the comprehensiveness of sports sanctions. Muldoon's adoption of the Gleneagles Agreement facilitated the success of the Edmonton Games; but the Agreement was framed in such broad terms that the obstinate New Zealand Prime Minister was left with considerable room to manoeuvre.

This set the stage for the Springbok tour of 1981, over which New Zealand society was badly split and deeply shaken. Many New Zealanders questioned themselves, and debated and fought with others, including members of their own families. Massive demonstrations greeted each match. An opinion poll taken in New Zealand during the tour showed that 49 per cent opposed the Springbok presence, while 42 per cent favoured it.[38] The key crisis point was on 25 July when hundreds of protesters occupied the rugby stadium in Hamilton, forcing the cancellation of the second match of the tour. While these events traumatised New Zealand, South Africans viewed this incident live on television (the first live rugby broadcast from overseas), and whites must have been rudely awakened to the depth of animosity felt by many New Zealanders towards their boys. Images of the New Zealand police beating protesters and fortress-like rugby stadiums behind barbed wire 'shocked the nation' in South Africa.[39] Confronted with such dramatic levels of hostility for the first time, Springboks returned from New Zealand with 'more enlightened views on race' and began to question the necessity of many apartheid laws.[40] Within South Africa, the tour also caused political tension as the liberal opposition party, the Progressive Federal Party (PFP), opposed the tour, making it an election issue. The spectre of the tour protests, combined with internal debate caused by the partial integration of Craven Week (see chapter 4), put rugby firmly on the agenda of debates about the future of South Africa. In New Zealand meanwhile, Muldoon and his government bluntly defended the minimalist interpretation of the Gleneagles Agreement on which their support for the tour rested, clearly violating the spirit, if not the letter, of the document.[41] At one point during the tour, Muldoon declared Gleneagles 'a dead duck', and asserted that New Zealand was sure to pull out of it.[42]

From 1981 to 1992 there were no official rugby tours between South Africa and New Zealand, and South Africa was isolated from playing IRB countries from 1984 until 1992. In 1982, the Commonwealth Games Federation adopted a Code of Conduct which gave the Gleneagles Agreement clear and tough guidelines, so as to preclude future threats to the Commonwealth Games (New Zealand and Britain abstained)[43]. Despite the Code however, in 1985, the NZRFU announced plans to mount another All Black tour of South Africa. This time though, the recently elected Labour government of David Lange vigorously opposed the tour, which was finally cancelled when New Zealand's High Court 'granted an interim injunction [at the last minute] arguing that . . . the tour would be contrary to the rugby union's statutory commitment to promote and foster the game'.[44]

Even this did not dissuade some rugby men in both countries from seeking to preserve their cherished rivalry, however. Secret negotiations were held behind the scenes to arrange for top New Zealand rugby players to tour South Africa. Louis Luyt, then head of the Transvaal Rugby Football Union (TRFU), invited thirty New Zealand players to visit South Africa as individuals who would then play South African teams.[45] The players secretly left New Zealand to the embarrassment of the government, the SARB, the NZRFU and the IRB, all of whom denied prior knowledge of the tour. That Luyt and some New Zealand players and officials would go to such lengths to arrange a tour provides clear evidence for the strength of South African–New Zealand rugby ties. Even the PFP supported the tour once plans were revealed, only lamenting the way in which it had to be arranged.[46]

This New Zealand Cavaliers tour was significant in that the Springboks won the series by three matches to one, temporarily restoring South Africans' rugby pride even if the Cavaliers were not officially the All Blacks. In 1987 the first Rugby World Cup was held and the All Blacks, including many former Cavaliers, swept to victory. New Zealand's triumph only a year after the 1986 tour precipitated commentaries on the relative strengths of the All Blacks and the Springboks, with many in South Africa lamenting the fact that the 'true world champion' could not be decided in a subsequent match between the two teams.[47] However, SARB president Danie Craven argued presciently that the effects of isolation had already eroded the Springboks' ability to compete against the top sides of New Zealand, France and Australia.[48]

Sanctions, rugby and change in South Africa

Clearly, the anti-apartheid sports boycott movement, in New Zealand and internationally, recognised the cultural and political significance of South Africa–New Zealand rugby links. Following South Africa's expulsion from the Olympics, these links became the crucible of the sports sanctions struggle for both the boycott movement and South Africa. Robert Archer and Antoine Bouillon, having described the 'constant skirmishing and subterfuges which [were] part of the modern South African [sporting] game' in the late 1970s and early 1980s, assert that 'the real battle has been in rugby – and the crucial battlefield New Zealand'.[49] From the mid-1970s, the effort to force the severing of New Zealand–South Africa rugby relations was the single-most important driving force behind the extension of sports sanctions internationally. The boycott of the 1976 Montreal Olympics, the adoption of the 1977 Gleneagles Agreement, the dramatic and widely reported events surrounding the 1981 Springbok tour of New Zealand, and the subsequent adoption in 1982 of the Gleneagles Code of Conduct by the

Commonwealth Games Federation, all originated in the controversy surrounding, and struggle to stop, Springbok–All Black rugby. It is thus fair to suggest that this rivalry was one of the more important factors in the popularisation and politicisation of the apartheid issue internationally in this period.

It is not just in its catalytic impact on the international campaign for sports sanctions that the New Zealand–South Africa rugby relationship contributed to external pressure for change, however. A distinction must be drawn between the impact of sports sanctions generally, and the loss of international (especially All Black) rugby ties specifically. There is little question that sports sanctions of all kinds hurt sports-mad white South Africans. However, it was relatively easy for them to rationalise and deal with their isolation from international table tennis, swimming, track and field, and even the Olympic movement itself. As noted in the previous chapter, these sports were governed by authorities in which Communist Eastern Bloc and 'radical' Third World national representatives could together muster solid majorities. Thus, isolation could be explained away in white South Africans' virulently anti-Communist world view as part of the Moscow-orchestrated 'total onslaught' against them.[50] Moreover white, and especially male and Afrikaner, South Africans simply did not care as much, or in the same way, about these other sports as they did about rugby.

Isolation from international rugby was a different matter, on both scores. The dominant rugby – playing nations – South Africa's great rivals – were white, predominantly European in cultural origin, and thus 'civilised' in white South African terms. They were the countries with which their historical links were most intimate, and whose company they most wanted to keep. Thus, cultural isolation from the British Isles, Australia and New Zealand was much more keenly felt than isolation from African and Asian countries, for example.

Furthermore, the loss of international rugby links, in contrast with many other sporting rivalries, was bound to have deep repercussions among Afrikaners in particular, at both the grass-roots and elite levels. At the popular level, rugby isolation was certain to shake the core Afrikaner electoral constituency of the NP. As a 1988 Australian Foreign Affairs Department report noted: 'White teams and supporters nation-wide, from major provincial organisations to the smallest hamlets, have seen the rugby country they firmly believe to be the greatest in the world increasingly excluded from the international game and, in the eyes of many, denied their rightful place at the top of the world league.'[51]

Beyond this, given the intimacy of the connections between South Africa's political elite, concentrated in the NP and the Broederbond, and the elite of South African rugby, this particular sanction was especially likely to undermine the collective confidence of this crucial dominant social group.[52]

If rugby constituted a particularly important cultural and political pressure point, Springbok–All Black rugby was its epicentre. This was most clearly illustrated with the 1981 Springbok tour of New Zealand. As discussed above, New Zealand–South Africa tours were traditionally viewed in both countries and beyond as the pinnacle of international rugby – the unofficial world championship. New Zealand was the one other country in which rugby had a comparable place of national cultural centrality to that which it held in South Africa.[53] In part because of this semi-mythical rivalry, as well as long and untroubled historical links through the British Empire and the Commonwealth, New Zealand was certainly regarded by white South Africans as among their oldest and closest friends. Yet in 1981, this old and comfortable friend, with its relatively isolated and placid society, was collectively traumatised by the Springbok tour. As South Africans watched these developments live and uncensored and read the press reports, there must have been a growing realisation, as there was in New Zealand, that there could be no further full international tours between these two great rivals so long as apartheid persisted. According to one South African correspondent:

> Final decisions about whether the Boks will tour again have been thrown into the court of the politicians. Much will depend on changes taking place in South Africa over the next few years and, clearly, if an objectionable form of apartheid still exists in South Africa when a Springbok tour is again at issue, the Boks will not be seen in New Zealand, or Britain for that matter.
>
> The traumatic events of the last few weeks have shown that a large body of New Zealanders, completely separate from the ill-informed, despicable group of violence mongers, will again rally to an anti-apartheid cause and I simply do not see a New Zealand Government, once all things have been considered, again allowing one.[54]

Indeed, this tour was one of the last official international rugby series (as opposed to watered-down rebel tours) involving the Springboks, and the last significant overseas tour by a major South African sporting team before 1992. Thus, the 1981 tour and its aftermath surely fuelled a deepening sense of cultural isolation among white South Africans which, over time, weakened their resolve to resist major political changes. The continuing poignancy of this issue is illustrated by the statement of an opposition member in a 1986 parliamentary debate coinciding with the rebel tour of the New Zealand Cavaliers: 'I am sure all members will agree with me on this – . . . we all look forward to the day when we can welcome an All-Black team, an Australian team or Welsh team, *inter alia*, as teams fully representative of their own countries, instead of their finding some clandestine way of coming into the country. How we long for that day!'[55]

It must be emphasised that the significance of these developments lay not simply in the *fact* of South Africa's isolation from the highest reaches of international rugby, but also in the *process* of political controversy and struggle by which this outcome was achieved. In this respect, the New Zealand government of Robert Muldoon ironically made a key contribution to building international pressure for change in South Africa, not by its leadership, but by its obduracy in defending the autonomy of its sportsmen and their right to compete against South Africa in rugby if they so wished. Every step forward in the extension of the boycott campaign from 1976 onward – the Gleneagles Agreement, the protests against the 1981 tour, the subsequent adoption of the Commonwealth Code of Conduct to clarify and police Gleneagles – was, in the proverbial phrase, like pulling teeth from Muldoon and his government. This is not the place for an analysis of Muldoon's motives in taking the stubborn stand that he did; suffice it to say that, as implied earlier, they had a good deal to do with domestic political calculations. However, each time Muldoon and his supporters were forced to concede a round, the sports boycott movement in New Zealand and beyond, as well as the allied South African non-racial sports movement, heightened their profile, their degree of politicisation and their determination to push on towards the complete dismantling of apartheid, as the necessary prerequisite for the elimination of racism in sport.

Thus, the spectacle of New Zealand society split by the 1981 South African tour, and the subsequent sense that no further tours could be mounted safely, had a significantly greater impact internationally, and in South Africa, than a quiet shelving of the tour would have had. Moreover, the impact of the severing of New Zealand–South African rugby links specifically, and the momentum of the sports sanctions movement generally, was sharply stimulated not because of, but rather in spite of, the actions of the New Zealand government.[56] Conversely, the *initiative* in extending international pressure for change through action to end Springbok–All Black rugby fell largely to the highly motivated, broadly based and zealous domestic tour opponents in that country.[57]

Implications for the study of international relations

The case of South Africa–New Zealand rugby relations, and their role in the process of mounting pressure for change in South Africa, holds a number of salutary lessons for students of international relations. We will briefly discuss three which, although not novel, are often dismissed or overlooked, particularly by realists in this sub-discipline of political science.

The first concerns the way in which we think about sanctions and how they work, particularly when emanating from less powerful nations. As suggested at the outset, the bulk of the literature concerning sanctions against South Africa was preoccupied with the prospects for effective *economic* sanctions. This emphasis is broadly characteristic of sanctions literature as a whole. It flows in part from the emphasis in this body of work on the *instrumental* purposes of sanctions – that is, the direct effect sanctions have in modifying the behaviour of the target.[58] A concern with the instrumental purposes of sanctions implies the need for a measurable calculus: X amount of sanctions pressure is likely to be required to produce Y change in the behaviour of the target. This approach is clearly illustrated by the findings of *The Sanctions Report* cited at the beginning of this chapter.

Economic sanctions are comparatively easy to identify and measure, and therefore lend themselves to rational (albeit usually inaccurate) calculations of probable impact. However, they typically require a large preponderance of power on the part of the sender(s) to be directly effective in this instrumental sense. Consequently, one relatively recent analysis of the sanctions policies of non-great powers suggests that, given the limited power resources of such countries, their sanctions are usually driven in reality by *symbolic* rather than instrumental purposes. In other words, they are not really expected to have an instrumental effect on the target at all.[59]

The effects of the severing of New Zealand–South African rugby links suggest a couple of alternative conclusions. First, although they are more difficult to measure and analyse, cultural (notably sports) sanctions can have a significant influence on the target society.[60] In this case, rugby sanctions arguably had a significant psychological impact on key groups within white South Africa, thereby eroding their will to resist other forms of external and internal pressure, and hastening the launch of the process of change. Furthermore, the massive protest greeting the 1981 Springbok tour, and the subsequent demise of Springbok–All Black touring, was viewed as an important expression of solidarity by the non-racial sports movement in South Africa itself, and thus bolstered internal resistance to the policies of the South African regime.[61] Thus, while rugby sanctions cannot be regarded as a source of *direct* instrumental pressure on South Africa, they were a significant longer-term and *indirect* stimulus to change.[62]

More generally, greater attention needs to be paid to cultural sources of vulnerability and influence – notably but not exclusively in the area of sport – in thinking about sanctions. When our analysis of the nature and efficacy of sanctions is broadened in this manner, we can see also that, in some situations at least, sanctions emanating from non-great powers *can* have an instrumental, rather than purely symbolic, impact on the target society – as they did in the case of New Zealand and South Africa.

Second, this case clearly demonstrates that in certain discrete international contexts or issue areas, small and generally weak societies can occasionally play roles of substantial importance. In other words, despite the general and understandable bias in the study of international relations towards an emphasis on major powers and dominant forces, influence is in fact exercised on a contextual or issue-specific basis; and countries which are small or weak in aggregate terms can be surprisingly influential where their specific capabilities or characteristics allow.[63] To overlook the role of small societies in world affairs, as is often done in the international relations literature, is therefore to risk misunderstanding or misinterpreting certain important international developments.

In this case, the potent cultural significance of rugby in both South Africa and New Zealand, and in their bilateral relations, made the former an important focal point for the international struggle against apartheid in sport. It also meant that the campaign to end South Africa–New Zealand rugby links, and ultimately the impact of their severance on white South Africans, were important elements in the steadily increasing effectiveness of external pressure for change in South Africa. In attempting to explain why the South African government initiated the current process of change, most observers would not intuitively look to developments in New Zealand as a significant element. Yet, because of New Zealand's status as a dominant world rugby power and South Africa's fiercest rival, the role of this distant, economically insignificant country of little more than three million people was remarkably important.

Finally, a third implication from this case concerns the importance of non-governmental actors and initiatives as sources of influence across national borders (indeed, across vast stretches of ocean!). This is not a new point, but it is one which bears repeating, given the tendency in international relations to emphasise activities and interactions at the level of the state. As discussed in the previous section, the initiative in the process of working to end New Zealand–South Africa rugby links lay primarily with a broad coalition of domestic groups in New Zealand, *in opposition to* the state. These groups were based in New Zealand and were to a significant degree motivated by concerns embedded in their own society (such as the role of rugby in underpinning patriarchal social relations).[64] They were, however, also very much connected with a transnational network of anti-apartheid groups – including the non-racial sports movement in South Africa and in exile. Beyond this, these groups were in harness with Commonwealth governments, notably but not exclusively from non-white member-states, pressuring the Muldoon government first to sign the Gleneagles Agreement and then to respect its intent.[65] The point to be stressed here is that what we have argued was a politically significant international development – the ultimately successful campaign to sever New Zealand–South African rugby links – was clearly driven by a broadly based domestic social movement, in opposition to the government of their country.[66]

Conclusion

The importance of sport in general, and rugby in particular, in precipitating political change in South Africa should not be overstated. The effects of the loss of rugby links with New Zealand were, we argue, essentially indirect and longer-term in nature, enhancing the sense of international isolation felt by white (particularly Afrikaner) South Africans, and weakening their resolve to defend their way of life. It is our contention, however, that the generally unexpected decision of the de Klerk government to enter negotiations for the ending of apartheid, beginning in 1990, cannot be understood without an appreciation of the corrosive societal and psychological effects of steadily expanding cultural sanctions. And of these, the loss of international rugby links, above all with New Zealand, were the most potent.

The sceptic will argue that, even if the foregoing analysis is correct in its assessment of the significance of rugby in promoting change in South Africa, this is a special case. No other society, it may be asserted, has been as widely and popularly disparaged as white South Africa; and no other society (except New Zealand and perhaps Wales) has shared the same passionate love for, and devotion to, its rugby. In one sense it is obviously true that the South African case is distinct. In a more general sense, however, aspects of the South African case are less unique than has often been assumed – something which is becoming more apparent as the spectre of apartheid fades into memory. Gross and systematic human rights violations in other countries are receiving more attention than ever before, and the use of international sanctions is increasing, as evidenced in the decision to impose sanctions, including sports sanctions, against the Serb-dominated Yugoslav government in Belgrade in the early and mid-1990s. South Africa's deep passion for rugby may be very nearly unique, but other countries have relied heavily on sports in building national cultural identity, and share a comparably strong attachment to their game.[67] Furthermore, where sport does not have comparable significance, other dominant cultural practices may have a similar degree of political salience. Thus, the lessons of this case are likely to resonate elsewhere. Small societies with distinctive strengths will periodically find themselves at the centre of important international political developments; sanctions involving dominant cultural practices – notably sport – need to be taken more seriously as a source of international influence; and domestic and transnational lobbies and social movements are likely to intrude ever more regularly into international affairs. For South Africa, however, a different set of questions now arise: what role will sport, and particularly rugby, play either in fostering societal reconciliation in this still deeply divided but collectively sports mad country, or in reinforcing historic divisions?[68] Either way, the prominence of rugby has certainly persisted, as we investigate in chapters 7 and 8. It is to the role of rugby in the transformation to a new South Africa that we now turn.

Notes

1 An earlier version of this chapter appeared in J. Nauright, (ed.), *Sport, Cultures and Identities in New Zealand* (Sydney, Australian Society for Sports History, 1995), pp. 67– 94.

2 D. Woods, *Black and White* (Dublin, Ward River Press, 1981), pp. 49–50.

3 A. Payne, 'The international politics of the Gleneagles Agreement', *The Round Table*, 320 (1990), p. 428. For a similarly modest assessment of the impact of sports sanctions, see A. Guelke, 'Sport and the end of Apartheid', in L. Allison

(ed.), *The Changing Politics of Sport* (Manchester, Manchester University Press, 1993), p. 168.

4 For a fuller development of this argument, see D. Black, '"Not Cricket": the effects and effectiveness of the sport boycott', in N. Crawford and A. Klotz (eds), *How Sanctions Work: South Africa* (London, Macmillan, forthcoming 1999).

5 For examples of solid academic analyses, see M. Doxey, *International Sanctions in Contemporary Perspective*, 2nd Edition (London, Macmillan, 1996); and D. G. Anglin, 'Ripe, ripening, or overripe? Sanctions as an inducement to negotiations: the South African case', *International Journal*, 45:2 (1990). For an excellent reconsideration of the case of sanctions against South Africa, see Crawford and Klotz (eds), *How Sanctions Work*.

6 Commonwealth Committee of Foreign Ministers on Southern Africa, *South Africa: The Sanctions Report* (London, Penguin, 1989), pp. 114–15.

7 For a detailed analysis of de Klerk and the National Party as they moved towards negotiations, see D. O'Meara, *Forty Lost Years: The Apartheid State and the Politics of the National Party, 1948–1994* (Johannesburg, Ravan Press, 1996). Not unlike many other writers on poltics in South Africa, O'Meara pays virtually no attention to the massively popular cultural area of rugby in his otherwise superb and compelling analysis.

8 For a compatible argument, see R. Nixon, *Homelands, Harlem and Hollywood: South African Culture and the World Beyond* (New York, Routledge, 1994), pp. 131–54.

9 *Rapport*, 1 March 1992, asked voters to consider what the NP had done since de Klerk began the reform process on 2 February 1990. One of the eight questions asked was 'Is ons sportmanne terug op die sportvelde van die wereld' (Are our sportsmen back on the sportsfields of the world?). See also Nixon, *Homelands, Harlem and Hollywood*, pp. 151– 2.

10 *Beeld* (Pretoria), 5 March 1992, reporting on the upcoming tour of South Africa by the All Blacks who would play a match in Pretoria at the Loftus Versfeld rugby ground on 15 August 1992. This was just twelve days before the referendum vote. The article also reported on the upcoming visits of the rugby World Cup holders, Australia, and of Italy and Romania.

11 P. Hain, *Don't Play with Apartheid* (London, George Allen and Unwin, 1971).

12 The celebrated 1905 New Zealand tour and 1906 South Africa tour are discussed in J. Nauright, 'Sport, manhood and empire: British responses to the New Zealand rugby tour of 1905', *International Journal of History of Sport*, 8:2 (1991), pp. 239–55; 'Sport and the image of colonial manhood in the British mind: British physical deterioration debates and colonial sporting tours, 1878–1906', *Canadian Journal of History of Sport*, 23:2 (1992), pp. 239–55; and L. Laubscher and G. Nieman, *The Carolin Papers: A Diary of the 1906–07 Springbok Tour* (Pretoria, Rugbyana Publishers, 1990). Also see the discussion in chapter 2 above.

13 R. Thompson, *Retreat from Apartheid: New Zealand's Sporting Contacts with South Africa* (Auckland, Oxford University Press, 1975), p. 2. The role of rugby in reinforcing patriarchal structures and gendered differences in both New Zealand and South Africa is significant and under-researched, but is beyond the scope of this chapter. See S. Thompson, 'Challenging the hegemony: New Zealand women's opposition to rugby and the reproduction of a capitalist patriarchy', *International Review for the Sociology of Sport*, 23:3 (1988), pp. 205–12.

14 Quoted in Thompson, *Retreat from Apartheid*, p. 2.

15 Woods, *Black and White*, p. 43 (emphasis added).

16 For a discussion of compulsory rugby in South African schools, see J. Evans, 'Time to kick compulsory rugby into touch?,' *Personality*, 16 July 1990.

17 S. Crawford, 'A secular religion: the historical iconography of New Zealand rugby', *Physical Education Review*, 8:2 (1986), pp. 146–58.

18 *Sunday Times* (Johannesburg), 15 March 1970.

19 *Daily News*, 2 September 1976.

20 Woods, *Black and White*, p. 47.

21 See J. Nauright, 'Myth and reality: reflections on rugby and New Zealand historiography', *Sporting Traditions*, 6:2 (1990), pp. 219–30.

22 For more on the Broederbond and sport in South Africa, see I. Wilkins and H. Strydom, *The Broederbond* (New York and London, Paddington Press, 1979), pp. 239–52.

23 This incident has been extensively reported, but for effects on Maori New Zealanders, see G. Nepia and T. McLean, *I, George Nepia: The Golden Years of Rugby* (Auckland, A. H. and A. W Reed, 1963), p. 26.

24 The 1956 Springbok tour of New Zealand has recently been associated with the end of the period of innocence in New Zealand society. For specific discussions of New Zealand and the impact of the tour, see M. N. Pearson, 'Heads in the sand: the 1956 Springbok tour to New Zealand in perspective', in R. Cashman and M. McKernan (eds), *Sport in History* (Brisbane, University of Queensland Press, 1979), pp. 272–92; J. Phillips, *A Man's Country: The Image of the Pakeha Male, a History* (Auckland, Penguin, 1987), pp. 82–5; W. Roger, *Old Heroes: The 1956 Springbok Tour and the Lives Beyond* (Auckland, Hodder and Stoughton, 1991).

25 For a good concise account of emerging protest in 1959, see 'The rugby tour and the Maoris', *Fighting Talk* (Johannesburg), December 1959, p. 16.

26 M. P. K. Sorrenson, 'Uneasy bedfellows: a survey of New Zealand's relations with South Africa', in *New Zealand, South Africa and Sport: Background Papers* (Wellington, New Zealand Institute of International Affairs, 1976), p. 53.

27 *Cape Argus*, 24 March 1960.

28 For examples of this, see Republic of South Africa, *House of Assembly Debates (SA Hansard)*, 8 February 1967, pp. 924–36.

29 *New Zealand Parliamentary Debates (NZ Hansard)*, 7 September 1965, p. 2527.

30 Richard Thompson recounts the story in *Retreat from Apartheid*, p. 52. He states that 'Distinctions were made between those of "Maori blood" who were welcome and the "full-blooded", "black" or "very dark" Maoris who were not ... between an All Black team with one or two players of "Maori blood" which would be allowed into South Africa and an All Black team with "five black Maoris" which would not'.

31 Sorrenson, 'Uneasy bedfellows', pp. 39–42.

32 *Rand Daily Mail*, 12 March 1973.

33 See Sorrenson, 'Uneasy bedfellows', pp. 46–9.

34 Quoted in the *Daily News*, 2 September 1976.

35 New Zealand Government White Paper, February 1973, p. 5; Sorrenson, 'Uneasy bedfellows', p. 61.

36 Cartoons in the New Zealand press during the campaign portrayed SARB President Danie Craven as Muldoon's running mate.

37 See A. Payne, 'The international politics of the Gleneagles Agreement', *The*

Round Table, 320 (1990), pp. 417–30; and D. Macintosh, D. Greenhorn, and D. Black, 'Canadian diplomacy and the 1978 Edmonton Commonwealth Games', *Journal of Sport History*, 19:1(1992), pp. 26–55.

38 *Eastern Province Herald* (Port Elizabeth), 31 August 1981.

39 *Eastern Province Herald* (Port Elizabeth), 31 August 1981. See also Nixon, *Homelands, Harlem and Hollywood*, pp. 146–7.

40 *Sunday Times* (Johannesburg), 11 October 1981.

41 See 'Springbok tour takes place and reaction to sporting contacts with South Africa continues', *New Zealand Foreign Affairs Review*, 31:3 (1981), esp. pp. 31–2; and Payne, 'The international politics of the Gleneagles Agreement', p. 424.

42 *Rand Daily Mail*, 29 July 1981.

43 Payne, 'The international politics of the Gleneagles Agreement', p. 425.

44 Payne, 'The international politics of the Gleneagles Agreement', p. 426.

45 *Die Burger* (Cape Town), 15 April 1986.

46 *Cape Times*, 16 April 1986.

47 A good example of this appeared in the *Cape Times* on 5 June 1987, under the headline 'Let Springbok 15 sort out the real champions'.

48 *Cape Times*, 22 June 1987. Craven stated that 'We need overseas tours to maintain our high ceiling . . . We are losing out on international competition and it has affected our rugby'.

49 R. Archer and A. Bouillon, *The South African Game: Sport and Racism* (London, Zed Press, 1982), p. 296.

50 On the alleged 'total onslaught' of South Africa's enemies, and the 'total strategy' formulated in response, see in particular R. Davies and D. O'Meara, 'Total strategy in southern Africa: an analysis of South African regional policy since 1978', *Journal of Southern African Studies*, 11:2 (1985).

51 'Race and rugby in South Africa', paper prepared by the Department of Foreign Affairs and Trade drawing on information provided by the Australian Embassy in Pretoria, *Australian Foreign Affairs Review*, 59:4 (1988), p. 140.

52 On the importance of international rugby to the South African political elite, it is both amusing and telling that, according to the Afrikaner novelist Andre Brink, former Prime Minister Vorster arranged to be interrupted every fifteen minutes during his talks with US Secretary of State Henry Kissinger to be given the score of an All Blacks–Springbok rugby match. See Archer and Bouillon, *The South African Game*, p. 2.

53 An argument could also be made for the similar pervasiveness of rugby support in Wales.

54 D. Retief, 'Curtain is drawn on overseas tours', *Cape Times*, 12 September 1981. This quote is interesting on a number of levels, not least in its reference to an *objectionable* form of apartheid – implying that a less objectionable form might still be sufficient to secure the reacceptance of touring sides from South Africa. See also Barry Glasspool, 'Desperate bid to save the tour', *Sunday Times* (Johannesburg), 26 July 1981. Remember that the 1981 tour matches were the first beamed live back to South Africa from overseas.

55 M. A. Tarr, PFP spokesperson on sport, *SA Hansard*, 16 April 1986, p. 3449.

56 Although the much more positive anti-apartheid role of the subsequent Lange Labour government of New Zealand should be reiterated.

57 For insiders' accounts of the activities of the coalition of domestic tour

opponents in New Zealand, see T. Newnham, *Apartheid is Not a Game* (Auckland, Graphic Publications, 1975); and Richards, 'Implications of the Springbok tour'.

58 See, in particular, D. A Baldwin, *Economic Statecraft* (Princeton, Princeton University Press, 1985). For a good discussion of this tendency in the sanctions literature, see K. R. Nossal, 'The symbolic purposes of sanctions: Australian and Canadian reactions to Afghanistan', *Australian Journal of Political Science*, 26 (1991), pp. 29–31.

59 See Nossal, 'The symbolic purposes of sanctions'. See also Nossal, *Rain Dancing: Sanctions in Canadian and Australian Foreign Policy* (Toronto, University of Toronto Press, 1994).

60 For a concurring view, see P. Davis, *In Darkest Hollywood Exploring the Jungles of Cinema's South Africa* (Athens, Ohio University Press, 1996), p. 180.

61 See Archer and Bouillon, *The South African Game*, p. 301.

62 For a fuller analysis of the influence of sports sanctions in the context of the broader sanctions movement against South Africa, see Black, '"Not Cricket"'.

63 On the issue-specific nature of power, see D. A. Baldwin, 'Power analysis and world politics: new trends versus old tendencies', *World Politics*, 31:2 (1979). See also D. R. Black, 'Australian, Canadian, and Swedish Policies toward Southern Africa: A Comparative Study of "Middle Power Internationalism"', unpublished PhD thesis, Dalhousie University, 1992, esp. pp. 210–16.

64 See, for example, C. Dann, 'The game is over', *Broadsheet* (New Zealand), 97 (1982), pp. 26–8; and Thompson, 'Challenging the hegemony'.

65 See, for example, *56 Days: A History of the Anti-tour Movement in Wellington* (Wellington, Citizens Opposed to the Springbok Tour, 1981), pp. 80–1.

66 For a brief but illuminating account of the role of social movements in world politics, see R. Pettman, *International Politics* (Boulder, Lynne Rienner, 1991), pp. 139–50.

67 G. Caldwell has written about the importance of sport in the development of national identity in Australia, Canada, and the (former) Soviet Union. See his 'International sport and national identity', *International Social Science Journal*, 34:2 (1982), pp. 173–84. Other examples of sport playing a crucial role in national consciousness and political life come readily to mind: cricket in the West Indies, soccer in a number of Latin American countries, etc. In addition, television interviews showed that the sanction that affected 'men in the street' in Belgrade most was the ban on the Yugoslavian team's participation in the European soccer championships of 1992.

68 For alternative evidence on this question, see 'Not ready for prime time, South Africa's rugby team hasn't won friends', *Newsweek*, 23 November 1992; and F. Bridgland, 'South Africa test future under threat', *Sunday Telegraph* (London), 15 November 1992.

Chapter 6

Rugby, politics and the
ambiguities of transition

By the latter half of the 1980s, the apartheid state and its socio-economic and cultural projects were locked into what, with hindsight, was clearly a terminal crisis. Yet neither the path out of this crisis, nor the will of the country's political leadership to find and take it, were at all clear. In the words of Dan O'Meara:

> After forty years in power, the National Party had come to recognise that its historic mission to impose apartheid on South Africa had failed . . . [T]he entire society remained imprisoned in the crumbling but still standing ruins of apartheid. Yet the NP government seemed completely unable to demolish their foundations, and clung to power with petulance and viciousness.[1]

Recognising the inevitability of profound political change, leading figures in South African economic, social and intellectual circles began to expand their contacts with opposition groups at home and in exile. Most conspicuously, first business leaders and then groups of prominent Afrikaners began to meet with the ANC in exile from late 1985 onwards, initiating the so-called 'trek to Lusaka'[2] (the location of the ANC's exile headquarters). These missions caused acute controversy at home but helped to build 'a groundswell for change within leading Afrikaner circles'.[3] Notwithstanding their cries of protest against these meetings with 'communists and terrorists', a handful of senior government officials themselves began to meet secretly with Nelson Mandela, helping to lay the groundwork for the negotiations to come.[4]

Sports organisations and policies were drawn into the vortex of crisis. Increasingly desperate for relief from the privations of mounting sports isolation, both the government and establishment sports bodies undertook a series of reforms and initiatives aimed at winning renewed international contacts, without challenging the legislative and social core of the apartheid order.[5] At the same time, they and the South African corporate sector orchestrated high-profile rebel tours, principally in rugby and cricket, designed both to bring relief from the pressures and uncertainties of late apartheid South Africa to their supporters, and to signal their defiance of their international tormentors. Yet such tours ultimately proved counter-productive, as they alienated foreign sports administrators disturbed by the disruption they caused and thus deepened South Africa's isolation. A notable example of this was the historic falling out between the SARB's Danie Craven and his long-time allies in the IRB as a result of the clandestinely organised tour of the New Zealand Cavaliers in 1986 – notwithstanding the fact that Craven claimed he had no knowledge of this tour until the New Zealanders arrived.[6] Nor could rebel tours effectively mask the country's painful isolation, as we have seen.

This destructive impasse in South African politics and sport broke with surprising rapidity in 1989 and early 1990, paving the way for the often-traumatic transitional negotiations between 1990 and 1994. Strategically, negotiations for sporting unity and the renewal of international competition played a distinctive and prominent role in the wider transitional process. They enabled the ANC and its allies in the Mass Democratic Movement (MDM) to signal to white South Africans both the immediate benefits and the larger promise of ending apartheid and embracing non-racial democracy. Yet, as sporting barriers crumbled with disorienting speed, many feared that rehabilitation was occurring too quickly, and that the faith of ANC and other negotiators in the unifying potential of sport was likely to prove misplaced without a much more committed approach to development issues in particular.

Characteristically, rugby held a place of special prominence in this process. As in the past, it initially led the breakthroughs towards change, but soon fell behind and ultimately trailed the process of sporting unity, thereby reinforcing its image as the most racist and recalcitrant of codes. Moreover, when rugby isolation finally ended and international competition was renewed, the behaviour of the sports establishment and supporters seemed to reinforce nostalgic and racialist identities, belying the arguments of those who saw sport as a force for breaking down social barriers and promoting unity. In this chapter, we look first at the manifestations of crisis in rugby which led key figures in the sport's leadership to take bold steps towards unity in 1988. We then trace some of the key events and issues in the process of negotiating unity, seeking to understand why rugby quickly lost its initial lead over other sports and achieved unity only tardily and controversially. The issue of rugby development will be considered separately, since it was a particular source of controversy at the time and will play a large role in determining the success of rugby's adaptation to the new South Africa. Finally, we assess rugby's potential to become a ghetto for unreconstructed Afrikaners bent on clinging to a nostalgic conception of their historic identity and role, concretely manifested in the 1992 Ellis Park test match against New Zealand that ended rugby isolation. This controversial test and its aftermath foreshadowed a future for rugby filled with ambiguity and uncertainty.

Establishment rugby's growing crisis

Coincident with the wider crisis of apartheid society, the late 1980s was a period of mounting anxiety and crisis for establishment rugby.[7] The SARB President Danie Craven's unflagging commitment to the good of South African rugby, as he understood it, meant above all the maintenance of international contacts and competition. Yet in the wake of the 1981 demo tour to New Zealand, this become ever more difficult. The last tour during apartheid by a major rugby power took place in 1984 when England came to South Africa. Competition was otherwise limited to rebel tours and, by and large, lesser powers – the Cavaliers tour of 1986 being the crucial exception. Often tours were possible only through subterfuge, such as competing against the (predominantly Argentinian) South American Jaguars, in lieu of official tests against the Argentinian Pumas, in 1980, 1982 and 1984.[8] And, when rebel tours were organised, as with the Cavaliers and the South Sea Barbarians in 1987, they paradoxically deepened South Africa's isolation as IRB members reacted strongly against the controversy they created. They were also tainted by the assumption that they involved substantial payments to the participating players in what was still a formally amateur sport. Ultimately, the two South African delegates to the November 1987 IRB meeting in Agen, France, Fritz Eloff and Jan Pickard, gave an undertaking that there would be no further rebel tours in the wake of the furore over the visit by the South Sea Barbarians, on pain of the SARB's expulsion.[9] Eloff and Pickard, ironically, defended the SARB as the 'amateur victims' who sought to protect rugby against voracious outside monetary interests.[10] It took delicate negotiations to secure the subsequent tour of an IRB-authorised World XV to mark the occasion of the SARB's centenary in 1989, during which allegations of player payments were rife. Indeed, many IRB officials knew that players were being offered large sums of money to tour in 1987 and 1988. Still, South Africa was not formally expelled. Players' and officials' reluctance to tour South Africa perhaps forced the SARB to resort to increasing financial inducements for tours.

According to noted rugby writer Stephen Jones, though the 1989 tour had the IRB's blessing, remarkably few players were available until South Africans bearing cash (provided by South African Breweries) arrived in Britain just prior to the tour. The Pugh Report, an investigation into corruption within the Welsh Rugby Union, concluded that at least one player had received £30,000 from the tour. [11]

Ironically, it was Craven, the staunch defender of rugby's traditions, and the SARB that did the most to professionalise rugby union in the 1980s through their support for rebel tours and complicity, at least, in the payment of rebel tourists. Both before and after the 1987 RWC, Craven and South African officials attempted to lure an Australian touring party. The potential players demanded to be paid to go. Meanwhile, a rebel Welsh team made up of past and present Welsh internationals went to South Africa. They threatened to leave the country during the tour unless they received additional payments. Undeterred by any potential fallout, Craven met with the Australian Rugby Union's (ARU) IRB representative Ross Turnbull during an IRB meeting in Hong Kong to discuss a possible post-RWC tour in 1987. The ARU backed out of the talks after failing to win support from the Australian government. Yet SARB officials still tried to lure an Australian team after the government and the ARU refused to offer official support for a tour. The First National Bank (formerly Barclay's) was prepared to bankroll an Australian tour to the tune of R10 million. Australian player representative Andrew Slack and his wife were flown to South Africa in December 1986 by Yellow Pages who were sponsoring a rebel cricket tour. Slack and fellow player David Codey returned to South Africa in August 1987, though by this time Craven had backed down from pushing forward with the tour.[12] Craven and the SARB then turned their attention to the SARB centenary in 1989, targeting a World XV. The IRB was complicit through its decision not to ban individual players from touring.[13]

South Africa's sense of rugby isolation was significantly deepened by its exclusion from the inaugural Rugby World Cup in Australia and New Zealand in 1987, and then again from the second World Cup hosted by the Five Nations[14] in 1991. The success of the 1987 RWC initially caused the SARB to react by intensifying its efforts to secure rebel tours rather than initiate negotiations for rugby unity. Indeed, as noted South African rugby historian Chris Greyvenstein put it, 'there was [at the time] a strong feeling that South Africa should leave the IRB and rely on rebel tours, regardless of the consequences'.[15] Many white South Africans denigrated these World Cup tournaments, arguing that South Africa would likely have won the 1987 event and that it could hardly be called the World Cup without them. Yet there could be no more telling or painful indicator of their increasing isolation than their absence from these events, which heightened rugby's profile and profitability world-wide. It is against this backdrop that Louis Luyt's petulant speech at the close of the 1995 RWC, during which he suggested that South Africa's narrow victory demonstrated the validity of their claims that they would have won the first two tournaments also, needs to be understood.[16] But along with this bravado, a growing number of South Africans, including Craven, expressed concern over the impact of their country's isolation on its standard of play. As the *Sunday Times* (Johannesburg) correspondent Mark Smit noted after the Springbok's narrow 20–19 victory over the World XV in the first test at Newlands in 1989:

> The manner in which their victory was won brought home the unpalatable truth to rugby-hungry South Africans. Without the cross-pollination of regular international tours, the Springbok game has become staid, cumbersome and unimaginative – lacking in thrust and authority, and terribly vulnerable to quick-thinking, fleet-footed counter attacks.[17]

It was the hunger for international competition, more than any other factor, which drove Craven and Luyt to contemplate a bold stroke in 1988 as rebel tours were becoming ever more difficult to arrange. With the SARB's 1989 centenary looming and South Africa's isolation more profound than ever, they realised that only a dramatic initiative would persuade the IRB to support a suitably auspicious event. They were thus receptive to ex-Springbok and noted liberal Tommy Bedford's suggestion that the SARB make contact with the ANC. It was this opening which set in train the process of negotiating unity in South African sports.

From rearguard to vanguard and back again: rugby and unity

It was Luyt who initially met with ANC officials in secret meetings, first in London and then in Frankfurt in May 1988. These meetings followed on from the work of PFP leader Frederick van syl Slabbert and Tommy Bedford, who had participated in an initial eminent persons' group to meet the ANC. Luyt's contacts set the stage in turn for the Harare meeting in October 1988, bringing together Craven and Luyt from the Board, the non-racial SARU's Ebrahim Patel, and Thabo Mbeki, Steve Tshwete and Alfred Nzo from the ANC.[18] At the meeting itself, the SARB and SARU representatives agreed to form a single non-racial controlling body for South African rugby, and the ANC in turn 'undertook to use its good offices to ensure that non-racial South African rugby takes its rightful place in world rugby'.[19]

This meeting provoked a furore in South Africa. The SARB executive committee split, with its Vice-President (and IRB Chairman) Fritz Eloff and several others criticising Craven for making a joint statement with what was widely regarded by white South Africans as a terrorist organisation. The minister responsible for sport, none other than then-Minister of Education F. W. de Klerk, condemned the talks and demanded a meeting with the SARB executive to express the government's disapproval.[20] While all contact with the ANC was controversial at this stage, particularly in light of the increasing tempo of activity in the (still-marginal) armed struggle, the level of controversy that accompanied this breakthrough meeting was surely heightened by rugby's close identification with the Afrikaner nationalist core in South African society.

The outcome of the meeting was paradoxical. On the one hand, it helped secure the World XV tour to mark the SARB's centenary. Indeed, Dobson quotes one top British official as saying that 'You should thank Dr. Danie Craven for the positive mood towards South Africa. The talks Dr. Craven and Dr. Louis Luyt held with the ANC in Harare last year made all the difference.'[21] Yet in large measure, because the World XV tour went ahead blatantly violating the sports boycott, the unity process between the SARB and SARU ground to a halt. Anti-apartheid sports activists could only oppose the tour and the organisation that had orchestrated it. This outcome clearly demonstrated the shallowness of the SARB's commitment to unity, and the instrumental calculations behind its decision to meet with the ANC. Talks about unity were valued only insofar as they helped achieve the goal of relieving South Africa's international isolation. It was this short-term attitude, based on a narrowly constructed conception of 'the good of rugby', which helped drop the sport from the front of the emerging race towards unity to the back.

The ANC, too, was sharply criticised for meeting with the SARB by some sports boycott advocates. Its decision to participate in the meeting, and commitment to facilitate the reintegration of a non-racial South African rugby body into world rugby, ran afoul of the long-held position of the umbrella organisation of non-racial sport, SACOS, that there should be 'no normal sport in an abnormal society'[22]. The SACOS position clearly meant that the sports boycott should be lifted only *after* the complete dismantling of apartheid.

Yet the ANC's decision to participate in the Harare talks and to under-take to assist in the renewal of international competition was not ill-con-sidered. Rather, it revealed an emerging shift in strategy, whereby unity within sport and the renewal of international competition ahead of the complete demise of apartheid would be used in an effort to win white support for the ANC and the wider process of change it sought to engi-neer. Sporting unity could be used to promote new social norms for a new South Africa, while international competition could serve as an inducement to whites to stay the reformist course.[23]

This shift in strategy was soon accompanied by important organisa-tional developments in the non-racial sports movement. While the SACOS had played a vital role in keeping the non-racial ideal alive within South Africa since its formation in 1973, its uncompromising stand on non-racialism had limited its appeal among African South Africans. For example, its refusal to deal with any organisation engaging in multinational sport, to allow the use of facilities requiring a permit under the Group Areas Act, or to countenance sponsorship from busi-nesses in receipt of government funds meant that it severely limited the sporting opportunities available to Africans living in impoverished material conditions and in remote locations dictated by apartheid laws.[24] Under the circumstances, and in light of the ANC's shift in strategic thinking, the conditions were ripe for a new, mass-based and more flex-ible anti-apartheid sports organisation firmly aligned with the MDM in South Africa. The upshot was the formation of the National Sports Congress (NSC), later the National and Olympic Sports Congress (NOSC) in July 1989. This laid the organisational groundwork for the negotiation of sporting unity – notwithstanding the continuing opposi-tion of the SACOS loyalists.

The NSC delivered the final push towards sports unity talks in response to a high-profile English rebel cricket tour in early 1990, led by Mike Gatting. The tour was 'a nightmare' for the establishment South African Cricket Union (SACU) and its leader, Ali Bacher.[25] Just months before, the rugby World XV touring South Africa had met with only limited opposition. The Gatting-led cricketers, by contrast, were met by NSC-organised demonstrations and disruptions on an unprecedented scale, harassing the English tourists at every step. On 14 February, less than a month after the tour began and less than two weeks after de Klerk's dramatic 2 February unbanning of the ANC, South African Communist Party, Pan Africanist Congress and other opposition groups, Bacher announced an agreement with the NSC to curtail the tour. Bacher and many other sports administrators had clearly got the message: future rebel tours would be too damaging and disruptive to be worth pursuing. The only path to international competition now lay through an accommodation with their non-racial counterparts. Rugby administrators, by contrast, either missed the full import of this message or were too stubborn to embrace it.

Unity negotiations were soon underway on a variety of fronts, including rugby. The basic conditions established by the NSC, under the influence of the ANC, were the acceptance by establishment sports bodies of the moratorium on international competition (a gesture of their sincerity and good faith); 'the creation of single, democratic, nonracial, and non-sexist governing bodies'[26] in conjunction with their non-racial counterparts; and an active commitment by the newly unified bodies to the eradication of inequality, involving an active development programme. While many commentators expected the negotiations to be long and arduous, they soon began to move forward with disarming speed, most strikingly in the high-profile arenas of cricket and the Olympics.

Ironically leading the way in light of the Gatting tour was cricket, under Bacher's politically astute leadership. By June of 1991 its establishment and non-racial bodies had united in a single United Cricket Board of South Africa (UCBSA), and by July the new body had won readmission to the International Cricket Council (ICC) in London (tellingly, the SARB was never expelled from the IRB). With the NSC's lifting of the blanket moratorium on international competition in October and the Commonwealth's lifting of 'people-to-people' sanctions at its Harare Heads of Government meeting later that month, the way was open to the renewal of official international competition. In what Rob Nixon has termed 'a half-apt yet utterly bizarre scenario',[27] the new era of international competition quickly began when South African cricketers, now rechristened the Proteas, toured India – the first country to impose sanctions on apartheid South Africa – in November 1991 as 'less controversial replacements' for the Pakistani side. In March 1992, South Africa participated in the Cricket World Cup in Australia and New Zealand, achieving a surprising degree of success in reaching the semi-final only to lose due to the tournament's strange rules regarding rain delays. Its presence in this tournament provided de Klerk with a superb propaganda vehicle during the whites-only referendum on the reform process that same month, allowing him to deal a 'sport-aided trouncing' to the recalcitrant right wing when 67.8 per cent of the white electorate voted to stay the reformist course.[28] Cricket's rapid normalisation, combined

with its high profile development initiatives in the townships, demonstrated a high degree of sensitivity to the new political winds blowing in
South Africa. It threatened rugby with ghettoisation as the sport of unreconstructed whites – a threat to which rugby's leadership was sensitive,
but poorly equipped to respond.

The ANC played a major role in negotiating cricket unity, specifically
in the person of 'Mr Fixit', Steve Tshwete. A member of the ANC's
national executive and later Minister of Sport in the post-1994 GNU, it
was Tshwete who accompanied Bacher to London to plead the UCBSA's
case for readmission to the ICC and before the High Commissioners of a
dozen Commonwealth countries.[29] Yet Tshwete was first and foremost a
rugby man from the Eastern Cape (he was President of the Island Rugby
Board in the course of his fifteen-year incarceration on Robben Island),
and he subsequently became closely involved in brokering an agreement
between SARB and SARU.

The other principal early breakthrough in sport rehabilitation
occurred in relation to the Olympics. Following a flurry of IOC study
visits in the first part of 1991 and the repeal of the the Land Act, the
Population Registration Act and other legislative pillars of apartheid,
IOC President Juan Antonio Samaranch announced the recognition of
the National Olympic Committee of South Africa (NOCSA) in July 1991.
This paved the way for the normalisation of South African relationships
with other Olympic-affiliated sports governing bodies, and for participation of an integrated South African team in the 1992 Barcelona
Olympics.[30]

With breakthroughs occurring on various fronts, the rugby negotiations became conspicuous by their tumult and tardiness. Not surprisingly, given rugby's historic identity and associations, it proved to be the
sport least equipped to adapt to the exigencies of the emerging post-
apartheid era. As discussed above, rugby took the early lead in the unity
sweepstakes with the 1988 Harare meeting; and notwithstanding the
friction caused by the 1989 World XV tour, a meeting between SARB and
SARU in February 1990 produced a decision in principle to form a single
non-racial national controlling body.[31] By the end of that same year,
however, talks had broken down in a welter of recriminations. The principal cause of their suspension was Craven's and the SARB's defiant
insistence that they would not abide by the moratorium on international
sporting links, and would indeed organise a (necessarily rebel) tour in
1991. In a late October 1990 statement, Craven reportedly insisted that
the SARB would in future 'take its own decisions on foreign tours and

would not be dictated to by anybody. He said SA Rugby Union chairman Ebrahim Patel was getting too big for his boots and he might call off the unity talks with SARU, whose word he no longer felt he could trust'.[32] Talks were in fact formally suspended in January 1991. While the immediate cause of the breakdown in talks was the SARB's rejection of the moratorium, and hence of NSC parameters for negotiation, the patronising attitude of the comparatively mighty SARB towards SARU and its office-bearers reflected in Craven's statement was clearly a major irritant. SARU's dismay over what it regarded as continued SARB poaching of its member unions deepened the rift.[33] Finally, the adequacy and sincerity of the SARB's commitment to rugby development for disadvantaged communities became an important source of conflict. This issue is taken up separately below.

The rugby negotiations were further complicated by increasing fractiousness within the SARB. Craven's falling out with the IRB as a result of the 1986 New Zealand Cavaliers tour probably weakened his authority,[34] which in any case he was wielding in a more erratic and irascible manner as he continued in the presidency through his late seventies and into his eighties. Moreover, any organisation which is led by the same individual for over thirty years is bound to develop some dysfunctional tendencies. Given Craven's legendary status, however, no one within SARB ranks was able or willing to challenge him frontally, even though much skirmishing occurred among pretenders to the throne. The growing divisions within establishment rugby became plainly obvious at its 100th annual meeting in March 1990, when two powerful provincial union presidents, Steve Strydom of the Orange Free State and Koos Vermaak of Eastern Province, were ousted from the executive, and the ever-mercurial Louis Luyt resigned from all SARB responsibilities in protest (his withdrawal was only temporary, probably to rugby's long-term distress, as we shall see). 'Board has become a farce', was the headline in a *Sunday Times* commentary on the meeting.[35]

The inevitable SARB–SARU accommodation was finally engineered in part through ANC intervention at the highest level. Tshwete intervened to get the talks restarted towards the end of February 1991 and was actively engaged thereafter.[36] As talks limped through August, he acknowledged the relative difficulty of reconciliation in rugby: 'Tshwete said that because rugby had been so heavily divided for decades and decades it was difficult to bring people together. He said the shedding of attitudes and associated problems had been far more complex than cricket.'[37] A significant part of the problem lay in the attitudes of many in the hard core of rugby supporters – the primary constituency of SARB administrators. Witness the racist and vastly ill-informed outburst of one audience member at a March 1991 Conservative Party by-election rally in Milnerton in response to Tshwete's intervention in the rugby talks: *'Wat weet 'n kaffir van rugby?'* (What does a kaffir know about rugby?).[38]

Ultimately, Nelson Mandela intervened in the process of negotiating rugby unity to inject some even higher level political impetus. Meeting Craven over breakfast at the home of Democratic Party MP Jannie Momberg in Stellenbosch, he reportedly promised to personally work to speed up rugby unity, asserting that 'unity would give further momentum to the peace process in the country'. Craven responded favourably, referring to Mandela as 'a man I can trust' and acknowledging the value of Mandela's and Tshwete's efforts in the unity process.[39] Progress was relatively rapid in the months that followed, and by early December 1991 both the SARB and SARU had approved the draft constitution of a new, unified South African Rugby Football Union (SARFU). The new body's executive committee held its first meeting on 19 January 1992, dividing representation on its dozen committees between ex-SARB and SARU people on a 50/50 basis. Officials of the old Coloured and African affiliates of the SARB, the SARFF and the South African Rugby Association (SARA), were unceremoniously dropped from the initial executive. Craven was made President of the new body for its first year, with SARU's Patel slated to take over the presidency in year two.[40] Minor hurdles remained – for example, over unity between the SARB and SARU affiliates in Western Province – but national executive structures were finally consolidated, six months or more after new non-racial governing structures had won readmission to international cricket and the Olympic movement.

The SARFU's official inauguration took place at its first annual meeting in Kimberley in late March of 1992. The meeting was supposed to be a celebratory occasion, heightened by the presence of NZRFU President Eddie Tonks and IRB President Sir Roger Vanderfield. Among the most newsworthy announcements of the meeting was the impending end of official rugby isolation, with home tours and tests against both the All Blacks and the reigning World Cup champion Wallabies from Australia scheduled for July and August. Some ten months after this inaugural meeting, in January 1993, the new body was rewarded by the IRB with the biggest prize of all: the right to host the 1995 Rugby World Cup.[41] Given the political uncertainties of this period, the IRB's decision was an act of faith over reason with regard to the country's future.

Yet even at this triumphal moment, there was reason for scepticism about the kind of unity that had been achieved, and the degree to which the new SARFU embodied a true commitment to non-racialism versus a mere reinvention of the SARB. In a critical commentary on the founding meeting in Kimberley, *South* correspondent Graham Abrahams argued that the leitmotif of the meeting could have been: 'We have come to bury Saru and praise Sarb'.[42] Rather than lay out a vision for the future, Craven's rambling forty-five-minute address reportedly dwelt on the 'tainted past' of apartheid-era Springbok sides. Notwithstanding the formal equality of SARB and SARU representatives on the SARFU executive committee, ex-SARU delegates had minimal representation among the provincial delegations at the meeting. On the twenty-two provincial delegations, there were only five former SARU delegates present.

At the senior leadership level, Patel did in fact take over the presidency when Craven died in office in early January 1993. He subsequently made himself unavailable for re-election in 1994, however, ostensibly because of conflicts with his professional responsibilities as headmaster of Lenasia Muslim School near Johannesburg. Why his dual responsibilities should have now become untenable after the years of complex and time-consuming unity talks is not clear, lending credence to Grundlingh's statement that 'whether this can be taken as a full explanation is open to question'.[43] Patel's withdrawal left the way open for the unopposed election of the chronically controversial ex-SARB stalwart, Louis Luyt. On this evidence, it is hard to disagree with Douglas Booth's assertion that, in rugby at least, 'unity was mostly a sham'.[44]

One of the core requirements of unity in all sports was the implementation of a credible development programme for players, coaches and facilities in disadvantaged communities. Development was a major source of controversy for rugby, both during and after the prolonged unity talks. What was the basis of this controversy?

The politics of rugby development

The roots of development controversy predate the unity battles of the late 1980s and early 1990s. For SARU negotiators and indeed the non-racial sports movement as a whole, true non-racialism and thus sport's putative healing role depended on an aggressive and determined effort to make opportunities for full participation available to all South Africans. The need for such an effort was beyond dispute: in 1982, the (South African) Human Sciences Research Council found that the white

15 per cent of the population controlled 82 per cent of the country's rugby fields; a 1984 University of Potchefstroom study found that per capita spending on white sport was between R7.13 and R19, while for blacks it was R0.82.[45] SARU representatives took the position that development had to be the top priority of any unified organisation.

This position implied that the SARB's previous development efforts had been completely inadequate. There were SARB and Craven loyalists who were deeply perturbed by this implication. The SARB had in fact authorised and undertaken many development clinics between 1982 and 1991, in which Craven himself was an enthusiastic participant. According to Paul Dobson, for Craven, they 'were a crusade . . . [T]he clinics, and all that went with them, became the main thrust of the last decade of his life'.[46] Indeed, despite his other shortcomings regarding issues of race and desegregation in rugby, Craven had been involved in so-called development initiatives at least as early as the 1940s as his occasional involvement with Coloured rugby teams in Cape Town attests. These were largely behind the scenes and personal efforts that did not lead to broad structural policies of development before the 1980s. During the 1982–91 period, claims Dobson, more than 314 clinics were held, attended by more than 88,000 players, while in 1991 alone, 40 clinics were attended by 16,500 players. Over the course of this decade, R11 million was reportedly spent on the developmental work of coaching, competitions and facilities.[47] The SARB's clinics were underway some five years before cricket launched its higher profile and widely praised development effort, and they were eventually supplemented by a series of new feeder competitions designed to encourage multiracial competition. As Craven saw it:

> We are building a new South Africa on the rugby field. We want the new South Africa to be experienced and to be observed on our playing fields, and if there is anybody who deviates from our ideals, he will be told there is no place for him [sic] in this new world.[48]

Yet critics such as Booth argue that the clinics were 'at best a paper exercise',[49] and the new SARFU was immediately beset by controversy over the inadequacy of rugby's development efforts. How are we to understand these apparently contradictory assessments?

Several fairly straightforward points can be made. First, while the figures cited above look quite impressive in theory, they were very small in relation to the needs they were ostensibly designed to meet. Second, and more importantly, the openings created by the clinics were inadequately followed up. While there is no doubting the dedication of the small team of principals in the clinics – Craven, Ian Kirkpatrick, Dougie Dyers and Piet Kellerman – or indeed the various other rugby types who periodically participated, even rugby officials acknowledged that 'the necessary follow-up operations were not made by provincial unions'.[50] Third, sustainable development efforts in disadvantaged communities were hard to achieve as long as the sport remained divided, with the majority of its supporters in these areas adhering to the ideals and affiliates of SARU, and with the SARB's organisational roots in such communities being so shallow. Indeed, given the bitter rivalry between the two organisations, there was no possibility of effective co-operation on development initiatives prior to unity.

Finally, and most importantly, however, establishment rugby bore the weight of its own history. As the sport most intimately associated with Afrikaner nationalism and carrying the heavy load of a century of racist ideological baggage, it simply had to try harder in order to demonstrate the sincerity of its commitment to development and its will to change. The shallowly rooted development clinics of the 1980s, weakly supported by the provincial unions, fell far short of this political requirement. Indeed, it is hard to avoid the conclusion that for many in establishment rugby, their support for development efforts was little more than a pro forma act aimed at obtaining the renewal of international competition. Nor were the development initiatives taken by the new SARFU from 1992 onwards sufficient to address this credibility gap.

No sooner had SARFU held its March 1992 founding meeting in Kimberley than it was immediately embroiled in a rancorous controversy over development. The instigator was Mluleki George, NSC President as well as a member of the disciplinary and amateur status committee of the SARFU executive. He was reported as saying on New Zealand television that the NSC 'would disrupt tours to South Africa because there was insufficient progress and money being spent on rugby development'.[51] Indeed, at the SARFU founding meeting, only R250,000 was firmly committed to township development, although in addition, 30 per cent of future tour and sponsorship revenues were to be allocated to development.

The controversy immediately put the SARFU executive on the defensive. They responded by outlining pending commitments for development totalling roughly R5 million from various sources. As the controversy continued, Louis Luyt threw his TRFU's financial weight around, turning over R2.1 million for development at the end of May with the injunction to 'get on with it'.[52] Yet throughout the prolonged controversy, the responses of key SARFU figures were revealing, insofar as new development spending was firmly linked to the impending tours, as Craven noted, 'we cannot finance anything without tours. If there are no tours, these plans fall away.'[53] While tour revenues would obviously generate new resources that could be devoted to development, the link made – no tours, no new development – clearly indicated the predominant hierarchy of priorities within the SARFU.

Goaded by continued criticism, SARFU finally launched an ambitious new development programme in March 1993, a year after its founding. In the subsequent year, R13 million was spent, 116,000 predominantly black rugby players attended clinics and coaching courses, and 6,000 coaches, 650 referees and 1,722 administrators country-wide helped organise and run the activities – a dramatic statistical improvement on the 1980s figures cited above.[54] Notwithstanding this unprecedented level of activity, however, rugby's development efforts continued to be plagued by controversy. Some events were marked by spectacular disorganisation, while there were reports of rugby officials bickering and jockeying for lucrative executive positions on development committees. Indeed, even during the new development programme's first year of operation, some observers were already voicing the opinion that with the World Cup in the offing, the programme was losing its urgency and administrators were looking upon it as a 'necessary evil'.[55] It remains to be seen whether the substantial commitments made in the context of the RWC will finally set rugby development on a more sustainable and less controversial path. What can be said of these early development efforts is that they tended to support the views of those critics who asserted that unity was, by and large, a shallow and elite-driven process, dominated by the priorities of the old SARB.

Moreover, the hope that sporting unity might play an important role in promoting national reconciliation and a pan-South African identity – on which ANC sport strategy was predicated – was sharply challenged by the Springboks' re-entry into international competition. Indeed, it is hard to imagine a more inauspicious and disturbing start to this new era than the 15 August 1992 Ellis Park test against the All Blacks.

Healer or divider? Rugby, nostalgia and identity

A central theme throughout this book is the importance of shared sporting practices and passions in forging strong collective identities. As the case of South African rugby illustrates, these identities can have considerable political potency. It is frequently tempting, therefore, for political organisations and leaders to try to utilise this identity-forming capacity for their own ends. Certainly the ANC, taking a leaf from the old Nationalist and Broederbond elite, has attempted to use sport in this way, although for very different, pan-South African purposes.

Yet, the identities generated in this manner are resilient, and can only be reconstructed over considerable periods of time. They are not easily amenable to political manipulation, and are often positively resistant to it. Indeed, nostalgic identities can reinforce a mythologised past, and run counter to a new nation-building project. The events surrounding the Ellis Park test of 1992 cast serious doubt on the notion that rugby could be turned to nation-building ends.

By the time of this historic test, ending South Africa's official rugby isolation, the country was well into what Dan O'Meara has described as the most dangerous six months in its history.[56] President de Klerk had been emboldened by his March referendum victory to reassert the NP's bottom line of power-sharing and group rights – a bottom line which the ANC could never accept. As tension increased, levels of political violence escalated dangerously.[57] In this climate of acrimony and recriminations, the negotiating process of the Convention for a Democratic South Africa (CODESA) broke down in May. Then, on 17 June, forty-three ANC supporters were massacred in the squatter camp of Boiphatong – another tragic and politically charged instance of black protesters being shot in a South African township.[58]

In the aftermath of Boiphatong, ANC representatives initially favoured a reinstatement of the moratorium on international competition, as Tshwete stated: 'The country is in a state of mourning. We will ask sporting bodies to reimpose the moratorium until the political situation is normalised.'[59] However, this quickly proved politically hazardous, as the first casualty of this decision was to be a series of soccer internationals against the Cameroonian national team – thereby penalising the most popular sport among blacks. When the Cameroonian authorities heeded the ANC call and cancelled the tour, black fans apparently jammed the ANC's switchboards demanding to know why 'their' sport was being forced to pay for the crimes of others.[60] Moreover, there was no guarantee that rugby and cricket governing bodies would act upon the ANC's call, potentially creating a situation in which sport reinforced, rather than reduced, social cleavages in South Africa. Quickly recognising the political dangers of seeking to reinstate the moratorium, Mandela intervened to have the Cameroonian tour reinstated, while the

ANC negotiated a series of conditions with the relevant sports governing bodies under which impending tours could proceed with its
approval. These included the requirement that a minute of silence
should be observed before matches out of respect for the victims of violence; that the old, white South African flag should not be officially displayed; and that the old apartheid anthem, *Die Stem van Suid-Afrika*,
should not be played. The agreements allowed the ANC to claim credit
for rescuing the renewal of sporting contacts.[61]

This neat political solution, however, naively assumed a measure of
goodwill from white rugby supporters which was not forthcoming.
Indeed, many were positively antagonised by the prospect of adhering to
conditions set by the ANC – an organisation which they had long
regarded as a band of 'communists and terrorists'.[62] On the day of the Ellis
Park test against the All Blacks, so charged with nostalgia and tradition,
large numbers of the 70,000 white fans came bearing old South African
flags which they flaunted. Conservative Party members exacerbated the
situation by passing out flags and leaflets encouraging the singing of *Die
Stem*. Inside the stadium, the assembled fans voiced their attitude
towards the ANC and its conditions by chanting, 'F... die ANC, F... die
ANC'. Climactically, when the crowd was asked for a few moments'
silence immediately prior to the game, they rose almost as one to sing *Die
Stem*. Adding insult to injury, the then TRFU president and SARFU executive member, Louis Luyt, approved the playing of the anthem over the
public address system at Ellis Park in an official expression of solidarity
with the crowd and defiance of his own organisation's agreement with
the ANC. Press reports in the days that followed captured the drama and
defiance of these events, and the intense controversy they generated. The
Afrikaans Sunday paper *Rapport* talked of 'softer tears of pride' and of the
Afrikaner's defiant will: 'here is my song, here is my flag. Here I stand and
I will sing today.'[63] The *Star*'s Shaun Johnson wrote that 'For that moment
inside the concrete bowl, it seemed like a besieged tribe had gathered to
take strength in their numbers and to send, from the protected citadel, a
message of defiance to their perceived persecutors.'[64]

How are we to understand the significance of these events? At one
level, they clearly demonstrate rugby's potential as a site for white nostalgia and cultural resistance and reaffirmation, in the face of disorienting and potentially disempowering change. Historian David
Lowenthal argues that nostalgia 'can . . . shore up self-esteem, reminding us that however sad our present lot we were once happy and worth-
while . . . nostalgia is memory with the pain removed. The pain is

today.'[65] For most white (particularly male) South Africans, nothing symbolised the success of their collective past more than the Springbok emblem worn by white national sporting teams, and above all the national rugby team. An informant in Vincent Crapanzano's 1986 book about white South Africans, *Waiting*, commented upon the relationship between rugby and white longing for the past:

> We've got to live now and plan a future for our children, but instead we live our past over and over again. A little while ago there was a program on television, the *Springbok Saga*, about our glorious rugby tradition . . . Whenever things get rough for us, we look to the past. We're out of international rugby now, and so we create a glorious tradition and watch it on television.[66]

The apotheosis of this storied past were Springbok–All Black tests. For decades, they had been treated by these two small, peripheral nations as emblematic of world rugby supremacy. Therefore, notwithstanding the fact that for the first time in the history of their rivalry neither the Springboks nor the All Blacks could claim to be the world's best rugby nation in August 1992,[67] there could be no more symbolically charged event for anxious white South Africans seeking reassurance in the past than the Ellis Park international.[68]

Even the location of the test, Ellis Park, could be viewed as a site or space for cultural resistance. The stadium itself was historically an icon symbolising the power of the white South African culture, economy, and planning and engineering. It was the largest rugby stadium in the world, symbolising for many whites the success of their culture and a space which they could control, at least when their Springboks played rugby. Both the old and new Ellis Park grounds, along with other hallowed test match venues like Loftus Versfeld in Pretoria and Newlands in Cape Town, were the scenes of legendary Springbok triumphs over the best teams in international rugby. They were thus tangible icons reminding whites of a nostalgic and successful past. It should come as no surprise, then, that the Ellis Park test produced such a patriotic outpouring, such an embrace of old white symbols, and such a show of defiance towards the black-dominated organisation which so imminently threatened their 'South African way of life'.

Yet the aftermath of the events at Ellis Park can also be seen as part of an often-painful process of learning and adaptation for many, though not all, white South Africans. While Luyt remained defiant in the days following the match, the SARFU executive committee issued a deeply apologetic statement designed to rescue the 22 August Newlands test against Australia. It expressed its embarrassment over the Ellis Park fiasco, apologised 'unconditionally' to 'anyone who has been offended by the breach', and – in a pointed rebuke of Luyt and the TRFU – ruled that in future, any union hosting an international test would have to agree, in advance and in writing, that conditions entered into by the SARFU would be strictly respected.[69] The ANC, for its part, issued a warning to rugby and its supporters before the forthcoming Newlands test: 'If the spectators go to the test not to watch rugby but to challenge the new South Africa the ANC will have no option but to oppose all future tours to and from South Africa including the 1995 World Cup . . . All spectators to the game stand challenged by this reality – they can make rugby a reconciler of people or they can use it as a ritual that cele- brates conquest and domination of black people'.[70] In the event, while South Africa suffered a record loss to the reigning world champions, the Australian Wallabies, the Newlands crowd recognised the import of the moment and behaved accordingly. They observed a period of silence for the victims of violence, while the host WPRFU adhered to all other ele- ments of the SARFU–ANC agreement. If rugby supporters had not expe- rienced a week-over-week conversion, they had at least begun to learn and accept the price of participation in the new South Africa.[71]

Conclusion

Just as it was possible to extrapolate from the Ellis Park test that rugby would remain the bearer of a nostalgic and racist national identity rooted in the apartheid era, so it became possible, briefly, to imagine that it was capable of performing nation-building miracles less than three years later. The joyous outpouring of support from virtually all segments of the 'rainbow nation' for the still nearly all-white *Amabokoboko* during their dramatic and triumphant RWC campaign enabled even the most cynical observers to imagine that deep divisions of culture and identity could be accomodated, even transcended, in the new South Africa – and that rugby could help this to happen.[72]

The euphoria did not last long. The World Cup triumph was followed in the next two years by a series of often-disappointing results and embarrassing retrograde incidents. These were capped in early 1997 by the 'Andregate' affair. Springbok coach Andre Markgraaff was forced to resign following the release of a secret tape of a conversation in which he appeared to blame the 'f...ing kaffirs' (by which he seemed also to mean the government, the NSC and Top Sport television) for his troubles.[73] The affair demonstrated the depth of casual racism in the senior reaches of rugby, and how little had really changed in its organisation – for as long-time rugby correspondent Dan Retief properly pointed out, Margraaff was not an aberration, but rather the product of an organisational culture which is 'aggressive, dictatorial, and hostile'.[74]

The incident and others prompted Tshwete's Department of Sport to launch a task force to investigate rugby's and Luyt's affairs in 1997. It also demonstrated that there is much continuity between the crowd at Ellis Park in August 1992 and the identity and culture of rugby's organisational leadership five years later. Yet as we will see in the next chapter, the events surrounding the RWC, and the admirable behaviour of many associated with the game in that period, underscore the fact that rugby has not been immune to the wider process of change, and is not without any capacity for more sensitive and enlightened behaviour. Rather, what emerged through the transitional period and continues today is a sport marked by deep ambiguity – a sport with a past which is at once glorious and shameful, which both attracts and repels. It is a sport facing a difficult and uncertain future.

Notes

1 D. O'Meara, *Forty Lost Years. The Apartheid State and the Politics of the National Party, 1948–1994* (Johannesburg, Ravan Press, 1996), p. 381. See also R. Price, *The Apartheid State in Crisis: Political Transformation in South Africa* (Oxford, Oxford University Press, 1991).

2 Price, *The Apartheid State in Crisis*, p. 238.

3 O'Meara, *Forty Lost Years*, p. 374.

4 N. Mandela, *Long Walk to Freedom* (New York, Little, Brown and Company, 1994), pp. 511–58.

5 See, for example, 'Race and rugby in South Africa', paper prepared by the Australian Department of Foreign Affairs and Trade, *Australian Foreign Affairs Review*, 59:4 (1988).

6 See P. Dobson, *Doc: The Life of Danie Craven* (Cape Town, Human and Rousseau, 1994), pp. 143–5. On sports reforms and the effects of rebel tours, see for example A. Guelke, 'The politicisation of South African sport', in L. Allison (ed.), *The Politics of Sport* (Manchester, Manchester University Press, 1986); and A. Guelke, 'Sport and the end of apartheid', in L. Allison (ed.), *The Changing Politics of Sport* (Manchester, Manchester University Press, 1993), pp. 157–9. Then SARB official Steve Strydom states that Craven knew about the tour ahead of time: 'Of course he knew, you would have to be naïve to think he didn't know', interview with John Nauright, January 1993. Thanks to John Baxter of the University of the Witwatersrand for setting up this interview.

7 Establishment rugby refers to rugby under the aegis of the SARB, including a coloured and an African organisation, but basically controlled overall by whites. Put simply, rugby controlled by the establishment.

8 Dobson, *Doc*, p. 172.

9 Dobson, *Doc*, p. 146.
10 D. Wyatt, *Rugby Disunion: The Making of Three World Cups* (London, Victor Gollancz, 1995), p. 108.
11 S. Jones, *Endless Winter: The Inside Story of the Rugby Revolution* (Edinburgh, Mainstream Publishing, 1994), p. 80; Wyatt, *Rugby Disunion*, pp. 108–9.
12 P. Dobson, *Rugby in South Africa: A History 1861–1988* (Cape Town, South African Rugby Board, 1989), p. 161. It must be remembered that this is the official SARB history.
13 Wyatt, *Rugby Disunion*, pp. 106–9.
14 England, France, Ireland, Scotland and Wales.
15 C. Greyvenstein, *Springbok Rugby: An Illustrated History* (London, New Holland, 1995), p. 247. Here Greyvenstein is referring to 1989, after the initial meetings between the SARB and the ANC.
16 See C. Simpkins, 'Luyt tackle that made the nation shudder', *Mail and Guardian* (Johannesburg), 30 June–6 July 1995.
17 Cited in *South African Sports Illustrated*, October 1989, p. 28.
18 In the ANC-led GNU, inaugurated in 1994, Mbeki became Executive Vice-President, Tshwete Minister of Sport, and Nzo Minister of Foreign Affairs. That such high-ranking officials should represent the organisation at the 1988 meeting indicates the importance the ANC attached to it. See Dobson, *Doc*, pp. 179–81.
19 *The Times* (London), 17 October 1988, cited in Guelke, 'Sport and the end of apartheid', p. 161.
20 For accounts of the meeting and its aftermath, see Dobson, *Doc*, pp. 179–81; Guelke, 'Sport and the end of apartheid', pp. 160–1; and A. Grundlingh, 'Responses to isolation', in A. Grundlingh, A. Odendaal and B. Spies, *Beyond the Tryline: Rugby and South African Society* (Johannesburg, Ravan Press, 1995), pp. 98–9. The reaction of de Klerk shows just how far political and sporting leaders had to go between 1988 and 1990 to set negotiations in motion.
21 Dobson, *Doc*, p. 181.
22 see C. Roberts, *SACOS: 15 Years of Sports Resistance* (Cape Town, author, July 1998); also D. Booth, 'The South African Council on Sport and the political antinomies of the sports boycott', *Journal of Southern African Studies*, 23:1 (1994), pp. 51–66.
23 On the ANC's new sports strategy, see B. Kidd, 'From quarantine to cure: the new phase of the struggle against apartheid sport', *Sociology of Sport Journal*, 8 (1991). See also D. Black, 'Not cricket: the effects and effectiveness of the sport against South Africa', in N. Crawford and A. Klotz (eds), *How Sanctions Work: South Africa* (London, Macmillan, 1998).
24 See, for example, Guelke, 'Sport and the end of apartheid', pp. 162–3; and Roberts, *SACOS: 15 Years of Sports Resistance*.
25 For a good description of this tour and its fallout, see Guelke, 'Sport and the end of apartheid', pp. 154–6.
26 Kidd, 'From Quarantine to Cure', p. 41.
27 R. Nixon, *Homelands, Harlem and Hollywood: South African Culture and the World Beyond* (New York, Routledge, 1994), p. 151.
28 Nixon, *Homelands, Harlem and Hollywood*, p. 152. See also Guelke, 'Sport and the end of apartheid', pp. 153–4.
29 'Ex-prisoner heads SA delegation at Lord's', *Eastern Province Herald* (Port Elizabeth), 23 May 1991.

30 See D. Macintosh, H. Cantelon and L. McDermott, 'The IOC and South Africa: a lesson in transnational relations', *International Review for Sociology of Sport*, 28:4 (1993), pp. 385–8.
31 'Rugby bodies agree to unite', *Cape Times*, 23 February 1990.
32 M. Shafto, '"I don't trust SARU", says Doc Craven', *Cape Argus*, 20 October 1990; see also L. Rulashe, 'Craven's alone in the wilderness', *Weekly Mail* (Johannesburg), 7 December 1990.
33 G. Abrahams, 'Unity's off!', *South*, 24 January 1991.
34 See Dobson, *Doc*, p. 147.
35 M. Smit, 'Board has become a farce', *Sunday Times* (Johannesburg), 11 March 1990; see also 'Shake-up at SARB as reps thrown out, Luyt quits', *The Citizen*, 10 March 1990.
36 D. Viljoen, 'Rugby unity: Craven meets the ANC', *Cape Argus*, 27 February 1991.
37 I. Gault, 'Rugby summit fails to speed up unity', *Sunday Times* (Johannesburg), 4 August 1991.
38 'ANC man called "kaffir"', *Cape Times*, 6 March 1991.
39 Reported in '"Man I can trust", says Doc after Mandela meeting', *Eastern Province Herald* (Port Elizabeth), 28 September 1991.
40 See W. van de Putte, 'SA rugby finally under one roof', *Cape Times*, 18 January 1992.
41 A. Grundlingh, 'The new politics of rugby', in *Beyond the Tryline*, p. 18.
42 G. Abrahams, 'Saru gets buried as a tainted Bok is raised', *South*, 28 March 1992.
43 Grundlingh, 'The new politics of rugby', p. 14.
44 D. Booth, 'South Africa: elite sport is winning', *Southern Africa REPORT*, November 1995, p. 28. For a detailed discussion of this position, see D. Booth, *The Race Game: Sport and Politics in South Africa* (London: Frank Cass, 1998).
45 Figures reported in Kidd, 'From quarantine to cure', p. 36.
46 Dobson, *Doc*, p. 214.
47 For an extended and sympathetic treatment of the SARB clinics, see Dobson, *Doc*, pp. 214–30.
48 Cited in Dobson, *Doc*, p. 226.
49 Personal communication with one of the authors, 6 June 1996.
50 E. Griffiths, 'SARFU expose the "development lie"', *Sunday Times* (Johannesburg), 5 April 1992; and Dobson, *Doc*, p. 222.
51 W. van de Putte, 'Peace pact?', *Cape Times*, 8 April 1992; and Griffiths, 'SARFU exposes the "development lie"'.
52 E. Griffiths, 'Luyt hands over R2.1m to fire SARFU development', *Sunday Times* (Johannesburg), 31 May 1992.
53 W. Steenkamp, 'Grassroots to gain from tours', *Cape Times*, 15 July 1992.
54 Figures from the *Star* (Cape Town), 16 August 1994, as cited in Grundlingh, 'The new politics of rugby', p. 6. The discussion in the following paragraph is largely derived from this source.
55 *Rugby 15*, October/November 1993, as discussed in Grundlingh, 'The new politics of rugby', p. 6.
56 O'Meara, *Forty Lost Years*, p. 411.
57 T. Ohlson and S. Stedman, *The New is Not Yet Born: Conflict and Conflict Resolution in Southern Africa* (Washington, Brookings Institution, 1994).
58 It should be recalled that the 1960 and 1976 New Zealand rugby tours of South

Africa occurred at the times of the Sharpeville and Soweto massacres respectively. See J. Nauright, '"A besieged tribe?": nostalgia, white cultural identity and the role of rugby in a changing South Africa', *International Review for the Sociology of Sport*, 31:1 (1996), note 2. Some of the discussion in this section draws from analysis in this article.

59 G. Evans, 'Back to the starting line', *Weekly Mail* (Johannesburg), 26 June–2 July 1992, cited in Nixon, *Homelands, Harlem and Hollywood*, p. 153.
60 Nixon, *Homelands, Harlem, and Hollywood*, p. 153.
61 G. Evans, 'A winning solution', *Weekly Mail* (Johannesburg), 3 July 1992.
62 Grundlingh, 'The new politics of rugby', pp. 10–11.
63 *Rapport* (Johannesburg), 16 August 1992, cited in D. Booth, 'Mandela and *Amabokoboko*: the political and linguistic nationalisation of South Africa?', *Journal of Modern African Studies*, 34:3 (1996), p. 467.
64 S. Johnson, 'Inside the protected citadel', *Star* (Cape Town), 17 August 1992.
65 D. Lowenthal, *The Past is a Foreign Country* (Cambridge, Cambridge University Press, 1985), p. 8.
66 V. Crapanzano, *Waiting: The Whites of South Africa* (New York, Vintage Books, 1986), p. 49.
67 The Australian Wallabies won the 1991 World Cup beating New Zealand in the semi-final and England in the final.
68 For an elaboration of this argument, see Nauright, 'A besieged tribe'. On the symbolic potency and controversy surrounding the Springbok emblem, see Booth, 'Mandela and *Amabokoboko*', pp. 461–6.
69 'Louis Luyt censured', *Cape Argus*, 28 August 1992; and 'Luyt refuses to apologise for anthem', *Daily Dispatch* (Cape Town), 29 August 1992.
70 African National Congress Press Statement, issued 19 August 1992.
71 Donald Woods had another explanation. With tongue partly in cheek, he put the difference between the crowd behaviour at Ellis Park and Newlands down to the difference between the 'true [rugby] afficianadoes of the Mother City and the yokels and yobboes of you-know-where' D. Woods, 'At least Newlands made good where Louis Luyt blundered', *Daily Dispatch* (Cape Town), 24 August 1992.
72 See also Booth, 'Mandela and *Amabokoboko*'.
73 'Tape of shame', *Sunday Times* (Johannesburg), 23 February 1997.
74 D. Retief, 'The rot remains', *Sunday Times* (Johannesburg), 23 February 1997.

Chapter 7

The world and South Africa in union?[1] The significance of the 1995 Rugby World Cup

The 1995 Rugby World Cup was the first major international event to be hosted by the new South Africa. Indeed, next to the April 1994 all-race elections signalling the start of the post-apartheid era, it was the largest and most widely celebrated such event in South African history. In the wake of the long years of mounting isolation, this simple fact was enough to make it a focus of intense public interest, within and beyond the country. Its significance, however, was compounded by rugby's historic associations with Afrikaner nationalism, apartheid, white privilege and racism. In short, the new South Africa's second great international coming out was to occur, ironically, with a tournament built around the historic sport of the oppressor.

This added sharply to both interest and apprehensions in the RWC run-up. Notwithstanding the emphasis that South African politicians and sportspersons of all persuasions had placed upon the potential nation-building role of sport during the 1990–94 transitional phase,[2] rugby seemed an unlikely candidate for the job. Its establishment administrators had been the most recalcitrant of all the major sporting codes in negotiating unity with their non-racial counterparts, and the virtually all-white Springbok teams had had a difficult time adusting both their game and their attitude to the demands of the post-apartheid, post-isolation era. Rugby's historic identity and associations were proving tenacious: the normally sober *Economist* (London) commented just prior to the start of the RWC that 'Rugby in South Africa is not just a white civil religion: it is the holiest ritual of the Afrikaner tribe.' It worried aloud that, rather than serving as a unifying event, 'the risk [is] that [the RWC] could do the opposite: re-open old racial wounds. Some of rugby's supporters are perched out on the unreconstructed wing of South African far-right politics. There could be jeering during "Nkosi Sikelel'I"'.

Despite many concerns beforehand, the tournament exceeded the expectations of its most optimistic backers. Notwithstanding various organisational and behavioural hiccups, it unfolded according to a fairy-tale script culminating in an epic Springbok victory over traditional arch-rival New Zealand in the tournament final. It launched a brief wave of transracial national patriotism, and became an extraordinary vehicle for the politics of reconciliation, practised most conspicuously by no less a past master than Nelson Mandela himself.

Yet the story is, of course, more complex and ambiguous than the celebratory mass-media accounts would have it. This chapter therefore explores the deeper significance of this critical case study[4] at three levels. The first is as a hallmark event, designed to facilitate capital construction, and international signalling aimed particularly at developing international tourism. The second, and in this case more important, level is as a crucial event in the politics of reconciliation and identity formation in the new South Africa – more particularly, we would argue, in the reconstitution of Gramscian-style hegemony. And the third, related level concerns attempts at fostering change in the organisation and identity of South African rugby itself.

Before developing these lines of inquiry, however, it is necessary to revisit the story of the 1995 RWC. This need not be done in detail, as it was covered in great depth by both the sporting and news media during the event; but the highlights set the stage for the analysis that follows. And there were plenty of highlights.

The Rugby World Cup story

The story begins with the awarding of the tournament to South Africa in 1992. According to Marcel Martin, one of the directors of RWC Limited – the private company established by the IRB to run the tournament – IRB delegates 'voted with their hearts' in taking this decision despite the violence and uncertainty of the South African transition.[5] As a result, considerable uncertainty surrounded the tournament right up until the successful completion of the 1994 elections, and most of the logistical preparations had to be compressed into a comparatively brief (one year) period of time.[6] Contingency plans were in place to move the tournament to New Zealand if the situation deteriorated in South Africa. This was at best problematic for the organisation of what had become the fourth largest sporting event in the world in terms of television viewing audience – more so since this was the first of the three RWC tournaments to be held in a single country.

Uncertainty, too, plagued the preparations of the Springbok side. Confounded by the effects of isolation, South Africa's re-entry into top class test play had been marked by startling inconsistency in play, and by controversy and recriminations among coaches, managers, selectors and administrators. Despite improvement from the level of play manifested in several sobering defeats of 1992, the Springbok side was not the World Cup favourite.

From the start, however, the RWC unfolded according to a best case scenario. In a savvy move, SARFU announced a decision one week before the tournament opener that all future age-group representative teams would be multiracial, with fixed quotas for players from 'underprivileged' (meaning black) backgrounds, beginning with the under-21 side which was to attend a tournament in Argentina two months hence.[7] SARFU's change in tone was to prove crucial throughout the tournament. Whether in direct response to this first gesture or not, President Mandela seized the opportunity of the RWC to promote racial reconciliation, visiting the team the day before their opening match against defending champion Australia at Newlands in Cape Town on 25 May. He encouraged the country to get behind 'our boys', notwithstanding the fact that the team (then minus its one Coloured player, Chester Williams, who was injured) was all white.

Prior to this, the Springboks and SARFU had adopted the slogan 'one team, one country' and, in a transparent and ironic public relations gesture, designated the traditional Ndebele and Zulu work song *Shosholoza* as their official anthem.[8] Following Mandela's own gesture and, even more so, the events of the opening match, these public relations ploys began to develop a measure of substance. The spectacular opening ceremonies elicited the following journalistic account:

> The Archbishop of Cape Town, Desmond Tutu, labelled South Africa a rainbow nation.
> During the Rugby World Cup opening ceremony, South Africa proudly gave a capacity Newlands crowd and a world-wide television audience of hundreds of millions a glimpse into the archbishop's meaning.
> The crowd was patriotic and passionate.[9]

While the ceremonies doubtless impressed the international audience, their effect was almost certainly most acutely felt by the large South African (particularly white) audience, presented with an elegantly packaged and emotion-filled panorama replete with stereotyped images of its own diversity. They were followed by a sparkling match in which South Africa upset the defending champions, sending much of the population into a joyful celebration. It was immediately and strikingly apparent that the celebrants included South Africans of all races – not simply (and predictably) whites. This prompted the start of a month-long discourse on the 'miraculous' nation-building effects of the RWC, exemplified by this early journalistic commentary: 'Rugby, long the religion of South Africa's whites, has performed an unexpected miracle – the conversion of blacks to the cause and the unification of the country behind a Springbok captain.'[10]

Also eliciting commentary – and arguably of even greater significance in understanding the effects of the RWC – was the behaviour of the predominantly white crowd at this and subsequent South African matches. Only three years previously, white rugby supporters had defiantly and provocatively flaunted the old flag and anthem and hurled abuse at the ANC and its leader during the Ellis Park test between South Africa and New Zealand which ended the rugby boycott.[11] During the RWC, by contrast, they enthusiastically embraced the symbols of the new South Africa and, in particular, the former 'communist and terrorist' turned President, Nelson Mandela.[12] Many faces were painted in the colours of the new flag, which vastly overwhelmed the (very) occasional old flag waved at matches. This remarkable if still superficial turnaround has to be understood, in turn, as a response to Mandela's own generous and genuine support for a team which he, along with most black South Africans, would previously have reviled.

The opening having been seized, the remainder of the tournament was marked not only by a succession of often dramatic matches, but by expressions of interracial reconciliation and generosity. Much to the delight of white South Africans, first Desmond Tutu and following the tournament Nelson Mandela called for the retention of the Springbok as the emblem of South Africa's rugby representatives, contradicting the long-held position of the non-racial sport movement and the NSC.[13] The rugby Springboks, in turn, endorsed the populist *Masakhane*[14] campaign in the week before the tournament final at the urging of Tutu. Finally, Mandela met the players again prior to the final against New Zealand in their change room, and then appeared before the super-charged crowd in a Springbok cap and jersey – an unimaginable sight only months previously. There followed a tense final between rugby's two greatest traditional rivals, won by a three-point drop goal in extra time; and a gracious acceptance speech by then captain François Pienaar's acknowledging the support of 'forty million' South Africans. The outcome prompted euphoric nation-wide celebrations which, in contrast with recent professional sports championship celebrations in North America and elsewhere, was marked by a spirit of goodwill and (in a society marked by violent crime) a virtual absence of destructive criminal activity.

There were, or course, lapses. In the first round, South Africa's match with Canada in Port Elizabeth was marked by the ugly 'Battle of Boet Erasmus', resulting in the expulsion from the tournament of South African hooker James Dalton and winger Pieter Hendricks.[15] It also prompted an incisive commentary by the author André Brink, commenting on the degree to which Afrikaner culture had come to celebrate foul play and hypocrisy both within and beyond sport during the apartheid years, and worrying that this trait was being passed on to South African society as a whole.[16] And, at the closing banquet for the semi-finalists and finalists, the chronically controversial SARFU President Louis Luyt displayed some of the bluster and arrogance which had marked the old South Africa, 'joking' that South Africa would/could (the exact wording was disputed) have won the first two World Cups had it been allowed to play, thus prompting a walkout by the English, French, and All Blacks before the main course was served.[17] His remarks must have rung even more hollow given that the Springboks survived by centimetres against the French in the semifinal and only defeated the 1987 champions, the All Blacks, after extra time. Indeed all three of the other semifinalists had beaten the Springboks at some stage in the two years leading into the RWC. On the whole, however, sour notes were infrequent, and what SARFU Chief Executive Officer Griffiths described as the 'feel good factor' prevailed.[18] How, then, are we to understand the deeper significance of this remarkable event?

The RWC as a hallmark event

Major sporting events are frequently associated with the desire of communities – national, regional and urban – to signal distinctive features, accomplishments and changes to a wider international audience. This signalling role has been particularly conspicuous with the Olympic Games: most recently, the Atlanta Olympics were conceived in part as a means of signalling Atlanta's decisive break with its racist past, as well as the emergence of the 'New South' as a dynamic centre of sophistication and high technology.[19] Prior to this, the Rome, Tokyo and Munich Olympics had sought to signal their countries' rehabilitation into the international community following their defeats in the Second World

War; while the Seoul Olympics were explicitly conceived by Korean leaders as an opportunity for the country 'to join the ranks of the advanced nations'.[20] Similar arguments were used by officials in Mexico in the context of the 1968 Olympics there.

Second order international events such as the RWC are generally not so prominently associated with, or effective at, this signalling role. In the case of the 1995 RWC, however, organisers and politicians clearly came to see the tournament as an opportunity to project South Africa's international rehabilitation, and its emergence as a multiracial, democratic 'rainbow nation'. This was reflected in the design of the opening and closing ceremonies, emphasising the diversity and richness of South Africa's multiracial, multiethnic cultural heritage. It was also reflected in the 'one team, one nation' slogan chosen for the Springboks and their adoption of *Shosholoza* as the team song. In some ways, of course, the juxtaposition of these images with the nearly all-white team and SARFU's white-dominated administrative hierarchy underscored how little had really changed, and how far the country had to go if its new identity was to become a more authentic reflection of the country's social hierarchy.[21] But as a declaration of intent, the signals sent were generally well and clearly received.

Thus, the RWC came to be understood as a hallmark event[22] – the first of its kind to be hosted, and exploited, by the new South Africa. Beyond the psychic and emotional benefits which such events are supposed to bring, there are several more material goals with which they are typically associated. In particular, they are justified by their backers – typically coalitions of politicians, businesses/sponsors and sports organisations – as vehicles for promoting the host as an international destination in the increasingly lucrative and competitive market for international tourism; and as a stimulus to socially desirable capital expenditure on sport and other urban infrastructure. Particularly since the 1984 Los Angeles Olympics, they have also sometimes been justified as profit-making enterprises in and of themselves – though often their profitability is seen as long-term and indirect.[23] Each of these motives and justifications was evident in the case of the RWC – though to varying degrees and with distinctive South African twists.

Because virtually all South Africans were so preoccupied with the transition and elections until the year before the RWC itself, it seems that many only awoke to its hallmark potential relatively late in the game. As a result, the benefits of the RWC were seen less as immediate and direct than as educative and indirect. In other words, South Africans could learn from the RWC where they stood in terms of their ability to take on events of this sort, and their readiness to meet the challenges of becoming an international tourist destination. There was a particularly sharp edge to these concerns in a country habituated to a diplomacy of isolation and unconventional, quasi-clandestine international intercourse. South Africans' self-analysis and preoccupation with international perceptions, as reflected in the English-speaking media at least, had an insecure, somewhat adolescent quality that was entirely understandable in the circumstances.

As a direct stimulus to international tourism, the RWC was something of a disappointment. From initial estimates of between 35,000 and 50,000 overseas visitors, actual figures eventually fell to around the 18,000 range, with the largest share bunched close to the final of the month-long tournament.[24] This led to a round of finger pointing just prior to the start of the tournament, involving accusations of administrative bungling and price gouging, between the SARFU's Louis Luyt, RWC Limited, and foreign and South African tourist operators.[25]

With hindsight, however, it may have been just as well that there were not more visitors, given the country's inexperience in dealing with such events. As it was, despite the overall success of the tournament, the RWC turned up a number of significant weaknesses in the South African service sector, which would have been exacerbated by greater numbers. While surveys showed that most visitors were reasonably satisfied overall with standards of service,[26] they found airports, fast food and above all public transport (no surprise to South African commuters) to be seriously sub-standard. These will be areas of critical importance should South Africa take on the hosting of larger events, such as the 2006 Football World Cup (soccer) or the 2008 Olympic Games – both active possibilities in the new South Africa's sport-focused global marketing strategies. The RWC helped give greater specificity to the conclusion of one consultant that, as matters stand, 'there is no way South Africa can presently handle the Olympics.'[27]

On the other hand, one area of considerable international apprehension – security – fared relatively well during the tournament. South Africans were sensitive to international press reports warning rugby tourists to beware of South Africa's high crime rate and extraordinary dangers.[28] In the event, however, police were able to claim that from their point of view, the RWC had been a 'resounding success', with only forty-two tourists reporting crimes in the course of the tournament.[29]

Overall, the touristic significance of the RWC lay in the fact that, by and large, South Africa was able to carry it off. Morever, it exposed South Africa to a total viewing audience estimated at up to 2.5 billion in 120 countries. The tournament did nothing, in other words, to discourage the upward trend in overseas tourists.[30] Indeed, it was sufficiently success-ful from an organisational perspective to enable South Africans to make a credible case that, with necessary improvements in key areas, they could carry off other major sporting events. It thereby set the stage for the pursuit of future hallmark events, possibly (notwithstanding Cape Town's failed bid for the 2004 Games) including the Olympics.[31]

A second major justification typically associated with hallmark events is that they provide a necessary stimulus for capital spending on new and rejuvenated sporting and urban infrastructure, which, argue civic 'boosters', is good for the community as a whole, notwithstanding serious questions concerning who benefits from such spending.[32] Indeed, these effects may be particularly important in the case of second order events such as the RWC – or the Commonwealth and Pan-American Games, for example – where the touristic benefits are more limited.

These justifications were offered in the case of the RWC. In particular, it was estimated that as much as R117 million was spent on projects to upgrade a number of the rugby stadiums around the country used in the tournament.[33] Nevertheless, the capital spending and infrastructural effects of the tournament were relatively limited. Indeed, one of the ironies of the event was that, due to the historically privileged position of rugby in the apartheid era, South Africa was uniquely well equipped with world-class rugby facilities. Thus, one of the distortions of the apartheid era contributed to the competitive success of this first major post-apartheid event.

As with its touristic effects, then, the infrastructural significance of the RWC was principally in underscoring some of the areas of strength and weakness in the country's existing facilities and ability to host major international events. It provided a good, relatively small-scale test run in an event South Africa was particularly well equipped to host, thereby facilitating the preparation of bids for other hallmark events.

Overall, the economic effects of the RWC were relatively limited, but beneficial. Total profits for RWC Limited were anticipated to be in the order of R110 million, of which a significant share would go to SARFU as the host union. The SARFU, in turn, pledged to use 30 per cent of its World Cup revenues for rugby development – an issue to which we will return below. And, while the direct benefits of the tournament to tourism were judged to be inconsequential in the final analysis, South Africa benefited from almost unprecedented international exposure and a relatively successful tournament. Moreover, some service industries, notably escort agencies, found that the influx of rugby fans produced windfall profits – just one indication of the important gendered effects of major sporting events.[34] But the significance of the RWC as a hallmark event pales in comparison with its role in the politics of reconciliation and the remaking of South African national identity. It is to this second theme that we now turn.

The RWC in racial reconciliation and identity formation

We have commented previously on the power of sport and sporting events to define and reinforce community – notably national – identities. As Grant Jarvie has noted, 'sport itself often provides a uniquely effective medium for inculcating national feelings; it provides a form of symbolic action which states the case for the nation itself'.[35] This is something which the leaders of the old South Africa clearly understood and attempted to exploit, as did their opponents in the course of what may be conceived of as a broadly based counter-hegemonic struggle.[36] Not surprisingly, then, the leaders of the new South Africa have been similarly sensitive to the potential power of sport in forging a new emotional, symbolic and ideological basis for South African nationhood.

It would obviously be a mistake to give too much weight to a single sporting tournament in the process of reimagining South Africa, no matter how dramatic its immediate impact may have been. Nevertheless, the RWC provided a historic opportunity – a dramatic moment – in which new, shared feelings and identities could be experienced, and new symbols advanced and embraced. To quote Jarvie again, it provided an extraordinary source of 'shared memories of specific events and personages which [may be] turning points for a collective or national history'[37] – one of the key constitutive elements of shared identity. Both South Africa's President and, as we shall see, the country's rugby establishment attempted to seize this historic opportunity to serve their political purposes – with some considerable success. Yet one must be careful in assessing the longer-term basis and impact of the identities thus advanced. What the RWC reinforced was the basis for a new hegemonic conception of 'South African-ness' which went some way towards defining a new basis for social consent, yet left underlying social and economic relations relatively untouched.

In order to understand this argument, it is important to identify the principle dynamics of the changes which occurred in bringing the whole country behind the 1995 Springboks. The main socio-political consequence of the RWC was that it encouraged and enabled the predominantly white, largely male rugby-supporting constituency to embrace the symbols, leaders, and idea of a new, multiracial, democratic country. It must be recalled that while white South Africans had clearly voted for a *process* of political change with their own 1992 referendum, the April 1994 elections had indicated that at that stage, they were far from accepting its concrete *outcomes*. Indeed, as Roger Southall has demonstrated, the vote in that historic election was overwhelmingly split along racial lines, with the vast majority of whites voting for parties (specifically the National Party and the Freedom Front) closely associated with group rights and, historically, the policies of apartheid.[38]

The RWC gave this politically and, more particularly, economically crucial group a historic opportunity to break with the symbols of the past – to complete the symbolic journey from the old to the new South Africa. It was able to do this because of the astute politics of reconciliation practised during the tournament, above all by President Mandela but also by the newly (and temporarily) enlightened administrative leadership of the SARFU;[39] and by the extraordinary generosity and enthusiasm of non-white – especially African – South Africans in embracing a sport, a team and even a symbol (the Springbok) which had been intimately associated with their historic oppression.[40]

Just who started this dynamic is difficult to say, and ultimately of limited importance since each step was essential in creating the overall effect of the tournament. Clearly the SARFU leadership, under Griffiths's influence, recognised the potential importance of the RWC in remaking its historic image. This recognition was reflected in its decision to implement affirmative action policies for age-group representative sides, in adopting the 'one team, one country' slogan, and in adopting *Shosholoza* as its team song. In particular, it sought to use this opportunity to regain lost ground – much of it forfeited to the more sophisticated and pragmatic leadership of cricket – in its quest for nation-wide popularity and support in the post-apartheid era.[41] But these steps would have rung hollow had not Mandela seized the moment to advance his own priority of national racial reconciliation. The President's embrace of the South African team as 'my sons', his appearance at the final in Springbok cap and jersey, and his post-tournament call for the retention of the Springbok in the light of rugby's role in uniting the nation[42] were extraordinary gestures of generosity towards white South Africans. They demanded – and received – a joyful reciprocal gesture from the predominantly white crowds at the matches and beyond.[43]

It has become clear that racial reconciliation looms large in Mandela's thinking – perhaps topping his formidable list of challenges and priorities.[44] He appears to have come to the not unreasonable conclusion that, without providing reassurance and a sense of belonging to white South Africans, the country's economic recovery and hence political transition and future cannot be secured. The danger, of course, is that in pursuing this priority, his government will exacerbate the alienation of its core black constituency.

The value of the RWC was that it enabled Mandela to reach out to white South Africans in a dramatic and extraordinary way without obviously running afoul of these kinds of trade-offs. In fact, quite the reverse: as noted above, one of the most striking aspects of the tournament was the extraordinary degree of support given by black South Africans to the Springboks. Dubbed by a leading black newspaper, *The Sowetan*, as the *Amabokoboko*, the South African side enjoyed an unprecedented degree of interest and support among the disadvantaged majority, well beyond the traditional black rugby playing strongholds of the Western and Eastern Cape. Notwithstanding a few over-enthusiastic journalistic accounts, there can be little illusion that the majority of black South Africans had become overnight rugby fanatics, as the SARFU leadership among others clearly recognise (see below).[45] Any doubt on this score was eliminated by the reaction of black South Africans to their country's equally triumphant performance in the African Cup of Nations (soccer) hosted by South Africa some months later, which made abundantly clear what the *true* national sport of the majority was. But the enthusiasm of black South Africans' support for 'their' rugby team was nevertheless striking – even inspiring. There could only be a tremendous sense of reassurance for most whites in realising that the changes wrought by April 1994, as limited as they were, had been enough to swing the vast majority of blacks behind a team, a sport, a dominant cultural practice which previously they would have reviled as belonging to their oppressors. For the price of supporting a new set of symbols, a new leader admired by the world, and a system of government which had made few material demands on their way of life – indeed promised a more secure economic future – they had gained a country in which they could feel comfortably at home. As sport commentator Jon Swift put it, 'intriguingly, the World Cup has brought the white minority closer to the ideals of our new democracy, by the almost unreserved support of all sectors of the community for the squad who espouse the ethic of "one team, one country," than any past political assurances.'[46]

Almost drowned out in the euphoria were the few critical voices which stressed the uncomfortable contradictions which this inspiring outpouring of unity was masking. Most obviously, of course, the team was nearly all white; but in addition, as Bafana Khumalo wrily noted, *Shosholoza* had traditionally been sung by black migrant labourers subject to super-exploitation in the South African mines, and while the South African players struggled awkwardly through *Nkosi Sikelel'i* they drew obvious inspiration from their lusty rendition of the old Afrikaans anthem, *Die Stem*.[47] The obvious, if curmudgeonly conclusion was that in the journey to this new epiphany of national unity, the road travelled by the white minority had been relatively short and painless, while the bulk of the distance had been covered by the newly enfranchised majority.

Put more theoretically, the RWC can be seen as an important instance in the re-creation of a hegemonic order in the new South Africa – an order in which class power is buttressed and legitimised through the active consent of most citizens, including those in subordinate groups.[48] Like many sporting events, and indeed more effectively than most, the RWC provided a set of 'uniquely gratifying'[49] shared experiences, memories and passions, linked in turn to a set of images and ideals around which all could unite. It helped to cement the support of the economically dominant white portion of the population behind the new political dispensation and its leadership; that is, it helped to forge a re-formed ruling coalition. And it engendered enthusiastic support among most black South Africans for a new South Africa which was little changed in material terms from the old.

It is, of course, unfair and inaccurate to suggest that nothing has really changed in the new South Africa. Clearly, the changes since the early 1990s have led to unprecedented opportunities for a minority of black South Africans, while the country as a whole is being governed with a degree of transparency and respect for fundamental human and political rights which is also unprecedented. Yet this is long way from the fundamental transformation of which anti-apartheid activists within and beyond the country spoke optimistically; and the order which is emerging, reinforced by events such as the RWC, seems to be retreating still further from these transformative ideals.

Similarly, it would be a mistake to suggest that nothing has really changed in the organisation and place of rugby in South Africa, and that the main role of the RWC was to relegitimise (temporarily, as it subsequently transpired) the status quo. Clearly, the tournament created progressive openings in the sport; yet it also strongly reinforced the dominant trend towards open professionalism and elitism in both South African and international rugby union. It is, then, to the significance of the changes wrought by the RWC on South African rugby that we finally turn.

The changing nature of Rugby in South Africa

The consequences of the RWC for rugby in South Africa seemed to pull the sport in two apparently contradictory directions. These trends were, in turn, both reflective and constitutive of contradictions in the ongoing South African transition as a whole, both nationally and globally.

On the one hand, SARFU seized the historic opportunity of the World Cup to attempt, however briefly, to reimagine its historic identity and to launch the process of remaking it as a forward-looking sport attuned to the norms of the new South Africa. These steps reflected, in turn, an understanding of the damage done by the sport's recalcitrance during the transition period. In the run-up to the World Cup, SARFU made a number of key personnel changes which gave the game a much more sensitive and polished public face, and advanced policies designed to bring it into line with the demands and expectations of the post-apartheid era. Chief Executive Officer Edward Griffiths, Manager Morné du Plessis, and Captain François Pienaar exemplified this new breed of leadership; but, despite his notorious outbursts,[50] President Louis Luyt also backed these personnel changes. Luyt seemed at the time to understand where the best interests of the sport lay, even if he often seemed personally incapable of putting this understanding into action. Griffiths candidly acknowledged that through the early 1990s, rugby unity 'had no visual expression', and that the sport 'did virtually nothing for development in those years'[51]. It should be noted that this was the case despite the best efforts of frustrated development officers such as Ngconde Balfour.[52] In 1992, Balfour and the National Sports Congress leader Mluleki George (later SARFU Vice-President) condemned SARFU for focusing on international tours rather than on development, a situation that was little changed by the time of the RWC.[53] The perception, Griffiths candidly noted, was that rugby 'wasn't really part of the new South Africa'. As a result, it lost standing and popularity compared with cricket in particular, whose leadership was much more pragmatic and politically astute.[54]

The most tangible and important expression of the rejuvenated SARFU leadership's programme to reverse this dangerous trend was a new commitment to rugby development within disadvantaged communities, marked by specific, concrete targets and resource allocations. In May 1995, Griffiths announced a new set of development programmes and commitments designed to give evidence of rugby's desire to remake itself as 'tomorrow's sport'.[55] Building on the SARFU's R16 million development budget for 1995 (30 per cent of its income), he announced that 40 per cent of the union's RWC profits – some R5 million[56] – would be devoted to development. Moreover, in order to increase awareness of, and participation in, the sport among black South Africans, he announced that in conjunction with all future Springbok training camps, the team would conduct a coaching clinic in an adjacent disadvantaged area. The SARFU would also establish a national Superkids project involving bi-monthly soft ball clinics in over sixty-five townships nationwide. In order to enhance opportunities for non-whites at the elite level, a policy of 50/50 black/white quotas for all age-group representative teams under 21 would be implemented, a policy remarkably similar to that advocated by Balfour in 1992.[57] Finally, Griffiths announced a programme to renovate and rebuild between fifteen and twenty rugby stadiums in townships around the country, starting with the NY 49 stadium in Gugulethu, just outside Cape Town.[58]

It is easy to be sceptical about these commitments given rugby's history, and Griffiths clearly anticipated as much. But even if some future administrators might like to back away from them, and even if it can be strongly argued that more should be done, it must be acknowledged that the setting of such concrete targets in such a highly public way marked a significant step towards the reform of rugby in South Africa. These and subsequent targets should serve as an important lever with which to pull the process of change forward, however much critics may question the sincerity of much of the rugby establishment. Yet another sign of the continuing effort of the post-RWC Springboks to forge a new identity for their sport is the ongoing effort to distance themselves from their more unreconstructed supporters, who insist on continuing to link the team to the symbols of the old South Africa. This was reflected in the August 1996 statement of then Manager Morné du Plessis: 'We [the Springboks] have decided to state unequivocally that the old flag is not a sign of support for the Springbok team. Every time the flag is flown it's an embarrassment to us. It's also disturbing to see the flag being flown because we've moved so far in the new South Africa.'[59] The battle to remake rugby is far from won, however; during international matches in 1996 and 1997, appearances of the old flag became more common. We will discuss rugby's post-RWC travails in the chapter 8.

The inverse of the relatively progressive and (in part) grass-roots oriented set of initiatives taken in the context of the World Cup was the dramatic announcement just prior to the tournament final of the sale by an alliance of the major southern hemisphere rugby unions of their exclusive television rights to Rupert Murdoch's News Corporation. The deal, for which Luyt was reported to have been the principle negotiator on behalf of his Australian and New Zealand counterparts, was worth US\$ 550 million and was to run from 1996 through to 2005.[60] It was negotiated and announced in some haste, apparently to pre-empt a spate of (professional) rugby league signings of top (ostensibly amateur) rugby union stars in the wake of the World Cup. These concerns were exacerbated by the News Corporation's establishment of the 'Super League' of rugby league in Europe and Australasia, causing a massive escalation of salaries and the establishment of rival rugby league competitions in Australia. It was rumoured that some players, such as South African scrum-half Joost van der Westhuizen, would be offered up to \$1 million to change codes. While representatives of the Australian, New Zealand and South African rugby unions denied at the time that their deal amounted to a 'unilateral declaration of professionalism' by the three southern hemisphere powers, the NZRFU Chairman Richie Guy remarked at the press conference announcing the deal: 'We are quite sure that the players ultimately will be very happy with the arrangements that have been made.'[61]

While the union representatives responsible for the deal were reluctant to acknowledge their sport's *de facto* abandonment of the amateur ideal, events shortly after the World Cup definitively exposed South African rugby's thinly disguised professionalism. Led by Pienaar, thirteen players rebelled from their regular Transvaal side, demanding a compensation package reflective of the escalating demands of their sport. The TRFU, also still headed by Louis Luyt, responded intemperately, to say the least, sacking the rebels. Only days later, however, the TRFU settled with the players on a deal very close to their original demands, in exchange for a contrite public statement by the players.[62] More to the point, though, it became crystal clear that players had been substantially remunerated for some time – an open secret in the rugby world. It came as no surprise, then, that in light of these and parallel developments in other parts of the rugby world, the IRB decided in August 1995 to officially end the sport's prohibition on professionalism.[63]

Thus, in the days surrounding the completion of the 1995 RWC, South African rugby moved decisively into an era of open professionalism, in which power seemed destined to shift decisively to multinational corporate media empires (which SARFU had obviously anticipated – indeed courted), and to individual stars (which the SARFU had obviously *not* anticipated). Although the 1995 RWC itself did not cause these developments – they had been gaining momentum for some years – it did provide a decisive push to the steadily expanding commercialisation of the sport which had been gathering steam since the first World Cup in 1987.

How is one to make sense of this development in relation to the grassroots development initiatives discussed above? What is likely to be their cumulative effect on the sport?

Rugby officials have argued that there is no contradiction between these two sets of developments. Indeed, Edward Griffiths argued that the unprecedented income from the Murdoch deal in particular would provide a windfall for the SARFU's development programme.[64] There is surely truth in this assertion; yet the sport into which new players will be initiated will be one in which control will have shifted sharply in the direction of multinational interests and priorities, and in which the emphasis will increasingly be on individual stardom and elite level professional teams and athletes. South African media interests, supported by much of the press, immediately cried foul when confronted with the Murdoch deal, and even threatened a constitutional challenge.[65] The crux of their argument was that in pursuit of profit, Murdoch might make rugby available only on internationally controlled pay-TV, denying access to less wealthy South Africans – an emotionally appealing argument, though an unlikely one in light of Murdoch's interest in maximising audience size and thus commercial revenue.[66] But regardless of these arguments, there seemed little likelihood that the deal, or the trend of which it was a part, would be reversed; indeed, it simply brought rugby belatedly into line with trends throughout the world of sport.

In the end, then, the fate of South African rugby in the post-RWC world would seem to run parallel to – and to be partly constitutive of – the fate of the new South Africa as whole. On the one hand, unprecedented opportunities for participation by the previously disenfranchised majority have emerged, and more and less sincere efforts have been made to redefine the identity of the game – albeit with national leadership still vested in the hands of segments of the old elite, slowly joined by a new multiracial element. On the other hand, just as these new opportunities are taking shape, overall control and direction of the game is increasingly slipping beyond South Africa, driven by the imperatives of competitive global capitalism in the television age. Rugby's transformative potential, like that of the new South Africa as a whole, is eroding in the face of increasingly intrusive global pressures, producing increasingly acute inequalities. South African rugby, and South Africa, are thus losing their exceptionality, for good and ill; they are being drawn into the transnational web of an increasingly global set of social and cultural forces. The impact of these forces in 1996 and 1997 and the decline of the SARFU and the *Amabokoboko* is assessed in chapter 8.

Notes

1 *The World in Union* was the title of the theme song for the the the Rugby World Cup: look for the CD *Anthems* from RWC 1995.
2 See, for example, the discussion of the sport in the African National Congress's *The Reconstruction and Development Programme* (Johannesburg, ANC, 1994). See also 'Sport helps reconciliation, Nelson tells medal winners', *Cape Times*, 17 May 1995.
3 'Rugby's new songs', *The Economist*, 27 May 1995.
4 See James F. Larson and Heung-Soo Park, *Global Television and the Politics of the Seoul Olympics* (Bouler, CO, Westview, 1993), esp. ch. 1, for a somewhat similar 'critical case study' of another major sporting event.
5 D. Retief, 'RWC Ltd as a business,' *Rugby World Cup Official Souvenir Programme* (Sandton, Ideadata (Pty) Ltd, 1995), p. 190.
6 See B. Spender, 'The World (Cup) according to Jamieson', *SA Sports Illustrated*, June 1995, pp. 76–8.
7 The team was to include at least seven players from such backgrounds. See D. Retief, 'SARFU to impose race quotas', *Sunday Times* (Cape Town), 28 May 1995. Achieving such a quota proved difficult in practice, as no black players were originally selected at the open trials for the under-21 tournament. The SARFU Chief Executive Officer Edward Griffiths persuaded officials to call another trial where some black players would be given a chance. Several were selected and on the basis of their performance in Argentina white selectors admitted that four black players would have been selected on merit had they been invited to the original trials. See E. Griffiths, *One Team, One Country: The Greatest Year of Springbok Rugby* (London, Viking Penguin, 1996), pp. 54–5. Also interview by David Black with Edward Griffiths, Cape Town, 11 July 1995.
8 The probable origins of *Shosholoza* are Ndebele. The song was sung by migrant mineworkers from then-Southern Rhodesia (Zimbabwe) as they marched down to the Witwatersrand gold mines. The main words of the chorus (trans-

lated) were, 'We are running through the hills of Rhodesia, we are running swiftly through the hills of Rhodesia'. Thus a song sung by mineworkers marching to harsh conditions and, in many cases, early death became an anthem of celebration for the new South Africa. Thanks to Christopher Merrett and his colleagues at the University of Natal for information on *Shosholoza*. For a biting commentary on this and other ironies associated with the RWC, see B. Khumalo, 'The voice of bitter reason" *Mail and Guardian* (Johannesburg), 30 June–6 July 1995.

9 'Spectacular pageant and a parade of 16 nations', *Cape Argus*, 26 May 1995.

10 A. Ferreira, 'Rugby performs a small miracle', *Cape Times*, 29 May 1995. See also Doc Bikitsha, 'The day the rainbow nation united behind the Boks', *Sunday Times* (Cape Town), 28 May 1995. One of the authors witnessed some of the celebrations in Cape Town on the evening following the opening match, and was struck particularly by the noisy patriotic displays of the taxis and their black riders.

11 J. Nauright, '"A Besieged Tribe"?: nostalgia, white cultural identity and the role of rugby in a changing South Africa,' *International Review for the Sociology of Sport*, 31:1 (1996), pp. 69–89.

12 See J. Smith, 'Non-events steal the show at Newlands', *Cape Times* Business Report, 29 May 1995.

13 A. Johnson, 'Keep Bok emblem for team – Tutu', *Cape Times*, 30 May 1995. With such powerful voices supporting the retention of the Springbok, the NSC subsequently had little choice but to acquiesce in this reversal.

14 An Nguni word meaning 'building for each other', – see B. Glasspool, 'Boks back campaign to build a better country', *Star* (Johannesburg), 20 June 1995.

15 Ironically, Hendricks's suspension enabled the only black player on the side, winger Chester Williams, to rejoin the team for the triumphant march to the final. This, we argue, may have been Canada's greatest contribution to nation-building in the new South Africa!

16 A. Brink, 'South Africa's dirty old habits die hard', *Mail and Guardian* (Johannesburg), 30 June–6 July, 1995. For a response, see A. Klaaste, 'Writing on the brink of doctrine', *Sowetan*, 3 July 1995.

17 The English team stood and 'openly scoff[ed] at the SARFU president' while within fifteen minutes of the speech, the English, French (the losing semi-finalists) and the All Blacks 'abruptly left the dinner, even before the main course had been served and returned to their hotels' See Griffiths, *One Team, One Country*, pp. 142–3.

18 Griffiths interview, 11 July 1995.

19 See J. Wong, 'New South tries to hide heritage', *The Globe and Mail* (Toronto), 1 August 1996.

20 Larson and Park, *Global Television*, p. 151, and more generally, ch. 6, 'The 1988 Olympics and the Transformation of Korea'.

21 Indeed black officials who had come into positions of power such as Ebrahim Patel, initial SARFU President, or those who sought to actively push the development process such as former development officer, Ngconde Balfour, were forced out of the SARFU. Remaining at the time of the RWC were Luyt, Fritz Eloff and Hentie Serfontein, President of the Northern Transvaal Rugby Union. After the Springboks, the most potent symbol of Afrikaner nationalism in sport during the apartheid era may well have been the Northern Transvaal team.

22 Hallmark events have been defined by Colin Michael Hall as 'major fairs, expositions, cultural and sporting events of international status which are held on either a regular or a one-off basis. A primary function of the hallmark event is to provide the host community with an opportunity to secure high prominence in the tourism market place.' C. M. Hall, 'The definition and analysis of hallmark tourist events', GeoJournal, 19:3 (1989), p. 263, cited in D. Whitson and D. Macintosh, 'Becoming a world-class city: hallmark events and sport franchises in the growth strategies of western Canadian cities', Sociology of Sport Journal, 10 (1993), p. 222.
23 For a good discussion and application of the idea of hallmark events, see Whitson and Macintosh, 'Becoming a world-class city'.
24 See Spender, 'The World (Cup) according to Jamieson'; Archie Henderson, 'Just the (wrong) ticket!', Cape Argus, 18 May 1995; T. Rawana, 'Rugby accounts for only 3% of tourists', Business Day (Johannesburg), 8 June 1995; and I. Hobbs, 'Agents slam SA hotels', Cape Times, 17 May 1995.
25 See, in addition to note 21, 'The World Cup's ticket hiccup' (editorial), and 'Luyt softens stance on Cup organizers', Cape Times, 17 May 1995.
26 A survey conducted by researchers associated with the University of the Witwatersrand Business School found that, of 400 foreign rugby visitors surveyed, 21 per cent found service standards 'excellent', 58 per cent felt they were 'OK', and 21 per cent found them 'bad'. S. Segal, 'Local service an Olympic hurdle', Mail and Guardian (Johannesburg), 7–13 July 1995.
27 Segal, 'Local service an Olympic hurdle'. The 2008 Olympic Bid was scrapped in 1998, however.
28 See 'UK press warns of SA danger', Cape Times, 23 May 1995.
29 'World Cup security a success', Cape Times, 5 July 1995.
30 'Running with the ball: the World Cup helps, but the broader picture is also looking good', Financial Mail (Johannesburg), 19 May 1995.
31 In addition, South Africa successfully hosted the Africa Cup of Nations soccer tournament in early 1996 after Kenya backed out, and will host the All-Africa Games in 1999 and the Cricket World Cup in 2002 among other international sporting events
32 Whitson and Macintosh, in 'Becoming a world-class city,' p. 237, rightly argue that 'We need . . . to question the claim that is often advanced but seldom demonstrated – that public money spent on subsidizing commercial sports and tourism produces returns for the community as a whole.'
33 'Running with the ball,' p. 24.
34 'Rugby fans flood city escort agencies,' Cape Times, 30 May 1995.
35 G. Jarvie, 'Sport, nationalism and cultural identity', in L. Allison (ed.), The Changing Politics of Sport (Manchester: Manchester University Press, 1993), p. 74. See also R. Gruneau and D. Whitson, Hockey Night in Canada (Toronto, Garamond, 1993), pp. 250–6.
36 On the Gramscian conception of hegemony and of counter-hegemonic struggle, see G. Jarvie and J. Maguire, Sport and Leisure in Social Thought (London, Routledge, 1994), ch. 5, 'Culture as a war of position and a way of life'.
37 Jarvie, 'Sport, nationalism and cultural identity', p. 76.
38 R. Southall, 'The South African elections of 1994: the remaking of a dominant-party state', Journal of Modern African Studies, 32:4 (1994), pp. 629–55.
39 The role of the SARFU's new Chief Executive Officer, former journalist Edward Griffiths, was important here: he was able to successfully change the

public face of the organisation in the run-up to the World Cup and to make the strategic moves which the old leadership increasingly recognised as necessary for the game, but seemed personally incapable of making. His subsequent sacking by Luyt proved to be a setback for the process of rugby rehabilitation in post-RWC South Africa.

40 See D Booth, 'Mandela and *Amabokoboko*: the political and linguistic nationalisation of South Africa?', *Journal of Modern African Studies*, 34:3 (1996), pp. 459–77.
41 Griffiths interview, 11 July 1995.
42 See M. Makhanya and N. Aitcheson, 'No quick decision on question of rugby's Springbok emblem', *Star* (Johannesburg), 27 June 1995; and 'We mustn't reward rugby for resisting change' (letters to the editor), *Sunday Times* (Cape Town), 9 July 1995.
43 'And the rainbow people chanted: Nelson! Nelson!', *Cape Argus*, 26 May 1995.
44 It has been suggested that the emphasis on reconciliation and forgiveness is generational. Raymond Suttner, an ANC MP and SACP stalwart, has said that the older generation (i.e., Mandela, Govan Mbeki and their cohort) are 'forever preaching forgiveness'. It would be interesting to explore the depth and roots of this generational priority. Author's discussion with Raymond Suttner, Cape Town, 2 June 1995.
45 See 'Up the Amabokoboko, say shebeen kings', *Sunday Independent* (Johannesburg), 24 June 1995; and '*Shosholoza* won't unite this arid town' (a story about Rustenberg), *Sunday Times* (Cape Town), 4 June 1995.
46 J. Swift, 'How rugby scored a try for the new South Africa', *Mail and Guardian* (Johannesburg), 23–29 June 1995
47 Khumalo, 'The voice of bitter reason'. See also J. Qwelane, 'Never mind the rugby, – it's the Mandela bit I want to sort out . . .,' *Weekend Argus* (Cape Town), 8–9 July 1995.
48 For a good discussion of the utility of the Gramscian notion of hegemony in understanding the socio-political role of sport, see J. Hargreaves, 'Theorising sport: an introduction', in J. Hargreaves (ed.), *Sport, Culture and Ideology* (London, Routledge and Kegan Paul, 1982). See also G. Jarvie and J. Maguire, *Sport and Leisure in Social Thought* ch. 5, 'Culture as a war of position and a way of life'.
49 The phrase is Jennifer Hargreaves's: see Hargreaves, 'Theorising sport,' p. 16.
50 See C. Simpkins, 'Luyt tackle that made the nation shudder', *Mail and Guardian* (Johannesburg), 30 June-6 July 1995; and C. Bryden, 'The man who can't avoid controversy,' *Sunday Times* (Cape Town), 2 July 1995.
51 Griffiths interview, 11 July 1995.
52 Indeed in 1992 and 1993, Balfour produced comprehensive development reports that outlined affirmative action plans needed to push the development process forward. These recommendations were not acted upon at the time, but resurfaced in the steps announced by Griffiths in 1995. See, for example, N. Balfour, *Development Report August to November 1992* (Cape Town, South African Rugby Football Union, 1992).
53 *Daily Dispatch* (East London), 5 November 1992.
54 Griffiths interview, 11 July 1995.
55 See 'South African rugby development', a statement by Edward Griffiths, Chief Executive Officer, SARFU, Cape Town, May 1995.
56 'Rugby Cup profits going to townships', *Cape Times*, 1 June 1995.

57 See Balfour, *Development Report*, where he advocates a 9 + 9 format of black and white players for all school level competitions. 'Competitions should be the meeting place and the market place for all our schools representatives, so that they may go home feeling proud of having been there, where there is no discrimination, no inferior or superior being, where nobdy comes from Guguletu, Soweto or Zwide, where nobody comes from Sandton, Rondebosch, or Summerstrand, but where everybody comes from South Africa and from Rugby.' 'Development of rugby', *Development Report*, p. 2.

58 This was in addition to the seventy-two fields the SARFU reported that it had built or renovated since 1992. Griffiths, 'South African rugby development'.

59 Cited in 'Springboks don't want "embarrassing" old flag at their games', *Star* (Johannesburg), 5 August 1996. It should be noted, however, that the Springbok side announced for a test against New Zealand at the same time as this announcement was made was all white, and mostly Afrikaner.

60 See, for example, D. Retief, 'Into a mega-Bok world', *Sunday Times* (Cape Town), 25 June 1996.

61 Cited in Retief, 'Into a mega-Bok world'.

62 See 'More Boks back rugby rebellion', *Cape Argus*, 6 July 1995; 'Luyt sacks rebel Boks', *Cape Times*, 6 July 1995; and Dan Retief, 'Player power wins the day', *Sunday Times* (Cape Town), 9 July 1995. The players asked for net monthly remuneration of R15000 from July to December; match fees of R2000 for a win and R1000 for a draw; and the negotiation of a medical aid scheme, a pension fund and a fund for the payment of disability benefits. These demands were far short of the inflated figures used by Luyt and his TRFU supporters in the PR battle preceding the settlement.

63 See, in general, *Rugby World*, October 1995; and, in particular, 'The report that changed the game', pp. 13–16 that issue.

64 Cited in Retief, 'Into a mega-Bok world'.

65 See 'Calling All Rugby Fans!' – a full page advertisement placed by M-Net in the *Cape Times*, 6 July 1995; also 'We stopped Lomu; can we stop Murdoch?', *Mail and Guardian* (Johannesburg), 30 June-6 July 1995.

66 N. Bierbaum, 'Murdoch's deal no cause for bleating', *Sunday Times* (Cape Town), 9 July 1995.

Chapter 8
Was the world in union too Luyt?
The decline and fall of rugby as a
nation-building force

The rugby authorities have in the space of 14 months, managed to turn a
national triumph into a national disgrace. And this is not because of a run of
three successive defeats against the New Zealanders (Jon Swift, *Mail and
Guardian*, 22 August 1996)

. . . the well being of rugby is of national importance. (Steve Tshwete, Minister
of Sport, 27 September 1997)

While the 1995 Rugby World Cup was tremendously successful in many
respects, the success of rugby as a nation-building force soon appeared
to be of little concern to the predominantly Afrikaner officials who maintained control of the SARFU at the top levels and of several large provincial associations. In addition to such attitudes, South African rugby
was soon faced with difficult adjustments in the game itself, as it belatedly went professional. Increased corporate interest accompanied professionalism. In 1996, the global trend of selling corporate naming rights
for sports stadia hit South Africa as the naming rights of Newlands were
sold to Norwich Life, and the stadium name was officially changed to
Norwich Park Newlands.[1] Similarly, Eastern Province sold naming
rights of their Boet Erasmus stadium to Telkom, and it was rechristened
Telkom Park.

In this chapter we examine the state of rugby near the end of 1997, over
two years after the RWC victory and less than two years before South
Africa defends its title in Wales in 1999. In the time since the euphoric
victory of 1995, the much-admired Springbok captain François Pienaar
was unceremoniously dumped, ostensibly due to injury problems, as
was the SARFU Chief Executive Officer Edward Griffiths via fax, with no
real explanation of his supposed shortcomings. Springbok coach Andre
Markgraaff was caught on tape making racist comments that many
believe reflect the persistence of racist attitudes among many rugby officials. He too lost his job as a result. Added to all these problems was a

competitive crisis caused by a record series of losses to the All Blacks, who defeated the Springboks five times in succession during 1996 and twice in 1997. Two of the 1996 defeats and both of the 1997 ones were in the new annual tri-nations home and away series between Australia, New Zealand and South Africa. The other matches in 1996 marked the first time that New Zealand had won a full test match series in South Africa. The All Blacks swept the first three post-tri-nations tests before losing the final one, again in Johannesburg. In 1997, the British Lions repeated the feat of the All Blacks, beating South Africa in a series at home for the first time since 1974 and the second time ever. Government officials distanced themselves from SARFU during 1996 and in 1997 and Sports Minister Steve Tshwete launched an investigation into alleged corruption and abuses within SARFU. Rugby officials initially refused to co-operate, prompting Tshwete to appoint a full judicial inquiry into SARFU following a similar investigation of South African soccer in late 1996 and early 1997. In this concluding chapter, we first discuss events subsequent to the RWC and then analyse these developments and those already outlined in earlier chapters in the context of the new South Africa and the present and future place of rugby in that society. We focus on three themes: the politics of identity and nation-building; the global political economy of sport; and rugby and national politics in the new South Africa.

From the RWC to professionalism

As we noted earlier, François Pienaar led the Transvaal rugby players in a strike against Luyt and the TRFU administration within a month of the RWC victory, demanding better working conditions and a share of the substantial profits in the game. Luyt, in his capacity as head of the TRFU, was initially determined to crush the revolt, but was ultimately forced to negotiate with the players. Soon after the strike, however, leading South African, New Zealand and Australian players were approached by a group calling themselves the World Rugby Corporation (WRC). The WRC wanted to start a global rugby union competition in which all players would be paid professional salaries amounting to hundreds of thousands of dollars for the top players. The WRC was ostensibly backed by Australian media mogul Kerry Packer, though he later pulled out of the deal. The world champion Springboks were crucial to the WRC plans, though it was apparent that Sean Fitzpatrick and many other leading All Blacks were signed up a well as most of the top Australian players. Again Pienaar was at the forefront of the WRC's strategy in South Africa. Pienaar secured signatures from most of the leading Springboks before Luyt got wind of the threat. Events moved rapidly in late July and early August with Luyt working hard to thwart a rugby revolution.[2] Led by national team captains – Pienaar, Fitzpatrick and Phil Kearns of Australia – many top players signed agreements with the rival organisation. At the last minute, Luyt, ably assisted by Griffiths, helped broker a deal that kept the Springboks loyal. Ultimately the Springboks seemed to still fear Luyt and decided to stay loyal to SARFU. The All Black and Wallaby players soon followed suit as for many it was an all or nothing proposition. As a result of the WRC threat, national level players in South Africa were put on contracts amounting to hundreds of thousands of rands a season, something unimaginable only a few years previously, despite large sums being paid to attract touring teams to play the Springboks during the second half of the 1980s. Among the leading Springboks from the World Cup, only Chester Williams remained a free agent. Soon after, on 27 August, the IRB voted to allow professionalism in rugby for the first time. Behind the scenes, rugby union was one sport of many in battles over media rights in Australia and internationally. Rupert Murdoch had bought the rights to broadcast the new tri-nations matches and the Super 12 southern hemisphere elite competition in 1995, and in 1995 and 1996 he tried to wrest Australian rugby league from Packer's control. The role of Packer in backing the WRC is thus not surprising and was part of the two media giants' battle for pay television rights in Australia. As Peter FitzSimons argues though, Packer's initial investment of a few million dollars with the option to pull out at any time (which he took) was a shrewd gamble. If the WRC came off, he would have a great televisual product. Murdoch by contrast had invested US$555 million over ten years in rugby union.[3]

The Super 12 and inaugural tri-nations series in 1996 was a huge success with large crowds and an exciting competition, at least until the test matches which New Zealand dominated. The winter of 1996 in South Africa was a rugby supporters equivalent of nirvana as the Springboks played home and away tests against the All Blacks and Wallabies before a full test match tour by New Zealand, their first official full tour of South Africa since the troubled days of 1976. Behind the scenes, however, Luyt was tightening his grip on elite rugby. Luyt's son-in-law, Rian Oberholzer, was appointed as the Chief Executive of South Africa New Zealand Rugby Inc. (SANZAR), the organisation running

Super 12 and the tri-nations series, and then as the SARFU Chief Executive Officer after the dismissal of Griffiths. Luyt also appointed his son, Louis Luyt Jr, as the manager of Ellis Park stadium. With Griffiths, the real architect of the successful 'One Team, One Country' campaign of the RWC, gone, the impetus for pursuing national reconciliation through rugby faded. One example of the new close-knit family leadership was suggested in July 1997 when the *Mail and Guardian* revealed that Luyt's son, Louis Jr, had received a large commission from the US$5 million sponsorship deal signed by the SARFU and Nike to sponsor the Springboks.[4] By the end of the 1996 series, the RWC team manager Morné du Plessis and coach Kitch Christie were no longer at the helm of the Springboks and the old Afrikaner establishment seemed in real control of the SARFU. Deals were struck in 1996 and 1997 that were so secret the SARFU Vice-President Mululeki George did not know the conditions. On top of these shifts back towards the old order, rugby supporters became restless over a string of losses to the All Blacks. Old South African flags began to reappear at matches as rugby seemed to be heading back to the laager[5]. Worse was to come. Pienaar, who carried injuries through much of the 1996 season, struggled to regain form. When new coach Andre Markgraaff was appointed late in the 1996 season, Pienaar was dropped from the captaincy and the Springboks. With du Plessis, Griffiths, and most strikingly for the public, Pienaar, gone, the 1995 RWC days began to seem a distant memory. After his failure to be selected for the Springbok team, Pienaar literally left to take up a contract to play professional club rugby in England.

In late 1996, Luyt faced his first serious post-unity challenge for the presidency of the TRFU from Brian van Rooyen. Van Rooyen, an accountant who plays at lock forward for his club, became concerned over the way the union's books were being kept and the centralised power that Luyt was keeping for himself and his family. Van Rooyen's concern, however, stemmed from a simple question he asked about rugby in March of that year: what had happened to the R7 million that was earmarked for black rugby development? When he received no answer as to how the money was being spent, he decided to pursue the matter until he had answers.[6] Luyt turned what could have been a discussion about the nature of rugby and its administration and future direction into a personal attack on van Rooyen.[7] After failing to defeat Luyt, van Rooyen was forced from his position as a TRFU Vice-President.

Van Rooyen's challenge brought home what many suspected, that leading provincial organisations and SARFU were not really interested in the serious development of black rugby. As Donald McRae recounts in the *Mail and Guardian*, Macdonald Masina is a good example of what is happening with development. Masina never played rugby until he was sixteen and his new Afrikaner headmaster said the school would play rugby instead of soccer. Masina said, 'we thought rugby symbolised apartheid . . . But when we heard that trips to Cape Town would be involved, it became more appealing'.[8] Masina's school became the only rugby playing one in Soweto and competed against white teams. Masina did well and was offered a scholarship to St John's, an elite private school in Johannesburg. He then played for Gauteng Lions B (the new name for Transvaal rugby) and the SARFU's 'Elite Development Squad'. He had not, however, been picked to play for Transvaal/Gauteng by July 1997. Indeed, up to that point, five years after rugby unity, neither Transvaal nor Orange Free State had fielded a single black player. Rather than pick Masina to play instead of the injured Hennie Le Roux in the final games of the 1997 Super 12 competition, Transvaal/Gauteng went to Griqualand West to secure the services of a white centre.[9] Even if in 1997 development was gathering pace and players like Masina and Sean Plaatjies, the latter depicted on the book's cover, were emerging, the perception was that white officials were reluctant to push too many black players forward at provincial and Springbok levels. As a result, the government, journalists and the wider public perceived that SARFU had become locked in some racist apartheid timewarp. Soon these suspicions were to be blown wide open. While the handling of the van Rooyen challenge did not help Luyt's public persona, another incident involving the national team coach and the handling of the incident by the SARFU put rugby in virtually the worst position imaginable within the new nation.

The Markgraaff affair: the racist tape and public perceptions of racism in rugby

In mid-February 1997, a tape of a conversation between then Springbok rugby coach Andre Markgraaff and former Griqualand West rugby captain Andre Bester, made by Bester on 22 October 1996, was played on the South African Broadcasting Corporation's national news. On this tape Markgraaff uses expletives and refers to the SARFU Senior Vice-President and NSC leader Mululeki George as a 'fucking kaffir', the latter a massively derogatory term used by some whites to describe blacks in South Africa during the segregation and apartheid eras. The

Mail and Guardian reported that the affair exposed an overpowering 'stench arising from the administration of South African rugby' and that the 'Markgraaff affair has given a glimpse of the shenanigans which seemingly go on behind the scenes' under the 'tyrannical' rule of Luyt.[10] Yet, the Markgraaff affair should not be surprising given the historical position of rugby and the fact that the predominantly white administrators within the SARFU now had to operate within new sporting structures that were quite different from those they grew up with during the apartheid era – even if in rugby union, the leading positions looked remarkably similar. While the RWC altered public perceptions of rugby for a relatively short time, many have not forgotten the connections of rugby with the apartheid state and with racist structures in old South African society. For many, Markgraaff's comments seemed to bring into the open what had been widely suspected – that the inner core of rugby had not changed despite the generous attempts of Mandela and the ANC to bring it into the mainstream of sporting identification in the new South Africa.

Too Luyt for SARFU? The government inquiries into the running of rugby in South Africa

Luyt's apparent rigid control over both the TRFU (now the Gauteng Rugby Football Union) and the SARFU to the possible detriment of rugby's public role finally prompted Tshwete to organise a Department of Sport and Recreation investigation into rugby, led by Director of Sport Mthobi Tyamzashe, and then to call a full judicial inquiry under Advocate Jules Browde and two other commissioners. Tyamzashe's task force produced a 730 page report to be incorporated into the judicial commission's work.[11] The terms of reference for the inquiry are listed in the table below.

The launching of a full judicial inquiry demonstrated the levels of mistrust which had come to exist between the government, the Department of Sport and Recreation and the SARFU and provincial rugby unions. As the opening quote to this chapter suggests, Tshwete and the ANC government viewed the role of rugby as vital to the nation-building process in South Africa. Rugby, via its administrators, could not, from their perspective, be allowed to revert to its apartheid roots. With charges of racism, nepotism and financial impropriety prominent in the public mind, rugby needed to be scrutinsed in the same way that Tshwete had soccer investigated in late 1996 and early 1997.

<table>
<tr><td colspan="1" align="center">Terms of reference for the investigation
into the state of South African rugby</td></tr>
</table>

• To inquire into and report on the financial, administrative and related matters concerning the management of rugby in South Africa by the SARFU and its affiliate unions, with a view to establishing whether such matters are being handled in a way that is constant with the best interests of the public and the rugby-supporting public in particular.
• To inquire into whether such matters are in the best interests of the game of rugby football, its development and its promotion among all South Africans, including those in under-privileged areas; and the principles of fair, open, honest and sound management, in particular.
• To inquire into the governance and functioning of the SARFU, including the SARFU's relations with the provincial unions.
• To inquire into the handling of present practices with regard to the development programmes in rugby; professionalism in rugby; intervention by administrators in team management and selection; the adequacy of the process of integration in rugby and its administrative structures; the employment and promotion of personnel; the awarding of contracts – especially those contracts relating to media coverage of rugby – payment of commissions and the awarding of any other benefit or privileges; sponsorship and the ownership and management of stadiums and other facilities.

Source: terms of reference as reported in the *Saturday Star* (Johannesburg), 27 Sept 1997.

The politics of identity and nation building: reading the decline of South Africa rugby

So what can we make of these seemingly unending problems in South African rugby and the SARFU administration? While it is clear that the 1995 victory created an unprecedented moment of national celebration and identification that crossed old colour barriers, it is perhaps too ambitious to expect a sport so linked to the history of apartheid and white racism to play a pivotal role in the building of a pan-South African identity in the new South Africa. This is even less likely when we consider that the top levels of the SARFU and several provincial administrations in 1997 remained in the hands of many Afrikaner officials such as Luyt, Fritz Eloff and Hentie Serfontein, from the apartheid era and old racially divided sporting structures. Indeed, their success in maintaining leading positions came during a time when most of the old leaders of the SARU were rapidly manoeuvred out of the new, supposedly unified structures.

This is not to say that there were no changes in rugby union. By 1997 development of facilities and the expansion of coaching clinics in some areas had begun to show results with Sean Plaatjies being selected as schoolboy Springbok team captain for the team's international match against Scotland at Loftus Versfeld in 1996. Plaatjies thus became the first black South African to captain an official Springbok team at any age-group level. Integration at top levels, however, was slow to come and affirmative action policies promoted by black development officials at the time of unity such as Ncgonde Balfour and by Griffiths in 1995 were met with resistance, as Griffiths recounts in his book, *One Team, One Country*.[12] At an under 20 tournament in Australia in the second half of 1997, the South African team was nearly one-third black, most of these players being Coloured; South Africa finished last behind Australia, New Zealand and Argentina. This demonstrates the crux of many problems at the top levels of South African rugby. The rapid integration of what are termed development players into top level teams is likely to see a short term decline in results as these players gain experience. Yet, as the record of Springbok supporters from 1992 to 1997 attests, many white fans are intolerant of change at the cost of their enjoyment of Springbok success.

The failure of sports officials and the ANC-led government, under the influence of such luminaries as Nelson Mandela and Desmond Tutu, to force a change in the Springbok emblem as originally agreed before the RWC has contributed to this reluctance to accept change as the entire history of Springbok triumphs is brought to bear by the media and success hungry supporters. Some of the uncertainties about change that led many rugby supporters to the outward and deeply emotional expression of their attachment to white cultural heritage at Ellis Park in 1992 remain, as economic problems persist and crime rises. Thus the nostalgic remembering of Springbok success may lead rugby down a path of becoming a site for white cultural resistance rather than a broad force for a new identification that appeared on offer in mid-1995. Indeed by 1997, with the increasing reappearance of old South African national flags and the perceived arrogance of white rugby officials, many justifiably believed that rugby was going back to the past rather than forward to the future.

Rugby could well fade further as a beacon of national identification in the national sports media market as the national soccer team Bafana Bafana qualified for the finals of the soccer World Cup in France in 1998. Indeed, Bafana Bafana, with four or five white players in its squad, is far more representative of the South African population than either cricket or rugby. In 1997, however, there was still a tendency on the part of white sports officials and media commentators to expect that black fans should be lured to the old sports of empire and apartheid rather than whites adopting the sport of the masses in a unified celebration of the new nation through sport. At least the cricket authorities correctly apprehended the need to change, dropping the Springbok emblem in favour of a new one. Rugby officials, by contrast, used the euphoria around the RWC victory to successfully lobby to maintain the old emblem rooted in the racist structures of sport during segregation and apartheid.

Ironically, it can be argued that the RWC in fact did a disservice to the cause of adaptation and change in South African rugby. The apparent uniting of the nation behind the nearly all-white Springboks, right up to the highest political levels, allowed rugby officials, players and supporters who were naturally reluctant to alter their familiar and cherished institutional and mental frameworks to believe that they did not need to – or at least that what they were doing already was enough. This respite from pressure for change created an opportunity for backsliding that led to the withdrawal from the sport of some of its most astute and enlightened figures – people such as François Pienaar, Morné du Plessis and Edward Griffiths. In a September 1996 article in the *Mail and Guardian*, former Springbok and initial unity negotiator, Tommy Bedford, suggested that 'Unless they start losing . . . That's the only time rugby structures will get changed, because while the results are OK then the public thinks that the way the game is run must be OK too'.[13] Developments in the aftermath of the RWC bear this analysis out. Yet the critical scrutiny to which the sport was being subject in the late 1990s may have come too late to enable it to successfully carve out a new identity and following as a sport of and for all South Africans – at least in this generation.

Rugby has been a central manifestation of the constructed collectivity of the white self in South Africa as represented in the Springbok rugby team. During segregation and apartheid, white rugby fans clearly saw the team as representative of the self, and blacks, by their very exclusion, as other. As such, the apartheid government placed great emphasis on the symbolic significance of Springbok rugby success. The continuing role of Springbok rugby in post-apartheid white imagining should not be under-estimated, though there are more fractures in white South Africans' imagined identification than before as many have genuinely worked to promote new structures and identities in South Africa. When Finance Minister Trevor Manuel announced that he supported the All Blacks rather than the Springboks in August 1996, not only did he face white public outrage but, remarkably, his comments sparked a sell off of shares on the Johannesburg Stock Exchange.[14] Yet many voices in the lively public exchanges that followed, particularly though not only from black South Africans, expressed support for Manuel's comments and thus their continued animus towards the symbolism of the Springbok.

South African rugby in the global political economy of sport

Rugby's role in the politics of identity in the new South Africa is likely to remain salient whatever the results of Bafana Bafana in the 1998 soccer World Cup for more than simply historical reasons. The Springboks have now signed a sponsorship contract with Nike worth a reported US$5 million and Rupert Murdoch's massive investment in southern hemisphere rugby ensures that the Springboks will receive significant local and international media coverage into the twenty-first century. Although there is support for the needs of sporting development in South Africa coming from the government and black sporting officials in particular, South Africa is firmly enmeshed in the global sports system, as we discussed in relation to the RWC as a hallmark event in the last chapter. Indeed the ANC government has fully embraced the hallmark event approach to sport and its links through tourism to wider economic development. The 1995 RWC was merely the first of a string of major international sporting events that South Africa will either host or attempt to gain the right to host. South Africa held the Africa Cup of Nations soccer championships in 1996 (won by Bafana Bafana) and will host the All-Africa Games in 1999 and the Cricket World Cup in 2002 among other international sporting events such as annual golf, tennis and motor racing events. The Cape Town Olympic bid for the 2004 Games failed, but it seemed probable in the aftermath of the International Olympic Committee decision that a bid for 2008 would be mounted. If such a bid is not pursued, it is likely that a bid to host the soccer World Cup for 2006 will be made, as this should go to either Latin America or Africa. As it has never been held in Africa, a South African bid should be competitive. Now that South Africa has been readmitted to the Commonwealth Games, it will certainly be in line to host this event in the near future. Indeed, Johannesburg has bid for the 2006 Games.

While there is evidence of economic benefits from the RWC, albeit much smaller ones than many anticipated, the Olympics are a very different proposition as many new facilities would have to be built at a massive cost. Major international events are now a standard part of 'boosterist' policies and developmental economics in countries with the infrastructure to compete on a global scale. As the only country in Africa with the potential to host large international sporting events, many politicians, capitalists and sports administrators have been drawn towards a cycle of events-driven development as one way to enhance the prestige and wealth of the new South Africa. Rugby will certainly play its part as South Africa remains one of the major rugby playing nations and will be likely to host the RWC at least once every 12–20 years. Additionally, annual matches with Australia and New Zealand and the Super 12 competition will receive extensive international coverage through Murdoch's global media outlets, as will test match series against other leading rugby playing nations. Rugby union may also soon become a full part of the Olympic programme again for the first time since 1924, creating further potential for South Africa in the sport. The 'boosterist' links to development of the South African economy are widespread. Reg Lascaris, in an article for the *Star* in Johannesburg argues that 'Every sports tour, every cultural exchange, every business foray should be a sell-South Africa event'.[15]

South African rugby faces a number of problems operating in the era of global professional rugby. While the SARFU contracts leading players, the weakness of the rand and the amount of money available for players overseas mean that the Super 12 teams and the Springboks may not retain the best South African players. By the end of 1996, stalwarts of the World Cup championship squad such as Pienaar, Joel Stransky and Rudolph Straueli had already taken up contracts to play professional club rugby in Britain. There is not a straightforward one-way outward flow from South Africa, however. South African provincial teams have attracted some leading players from Argentina, Australia and France for the Currie Cup competition. The rules of international rugby prevent transnational migrant players from playing for two different national teams, however, except in special circumstances such as exist between Western Samoa and New Zealand. The full implications of this new trend towards international player migration in rugby will take some time to become apparent – in South Africa and elsewhere – although it is possible to imagine economic and/or political circumstances in contemporary South Africa which could prompt a damaging exodus of top-class players.

The failure of the Springboks to achieve a high level of success in the new South Africa may lead to reforms in the organisation of rugby and decrease its significance to the white population specifically and the nation-building process in general – though the global connections and economic influences now at work make such a scenario less likely. It is clear that by 1997, the ANC government had developed a different approach to the game than Mandela had proffered in 1995. Yet, despite such changes to the government's approach, it is clear that the ANC has attached similar significance to the use of elite sport and sporting success as did the old National Party government. Indeed, its attempts to promote rugby and national identification in 1995 resonated closely with NP strategies in the past, though this time the entire population of the space identified as South Africa was to be included. Similarly, it is clear that the government firmly supports the use of international sporting events and connections as a major developmental strategy. It, too, will therefore find itself conflicted if the implications of a more profound reorganisation of rugby should prove to include a sustained decline in its performance and therefore international identification. The danger is that it will soft-pedal the need for change as a result.

Rugby and politics in the new South Africa

Since the RWC, Mandela, Tshwete and other ANC leaders have slowly distanced themselves from the Springboks. And, as we have seen, Finance Minister Trevor Manuel even went so far as to publicly admit that he supported the All Blacks against the Springboks, leading to widespread calls from whites for his resignation. The furore generated by this incident at the time exceeded any criticisms of his handling of economic policy. The failure of rugby officials to follow-up on the tremendous, broadly based appeal generated by the 1995 win, the unseemly concentration of control of the sport in the hands of Luyt and his family and continued arrogance on the part of some officials led Tshwete to use his position as Sports Minister to launch official investigations into rugby's affairs. So, although rugby does not have the intimate connections to the South African state that it had during the apartheid era, it nevertheless remains an important and emotionally charged cultural activity for many South Africans and thus an important concern of state policy-makers.

Moreover, the government's priority of reconciliation with whites remains a pressing one, and rugby a symbolically potent area in which to advance or impair it. If ANC policy-makers are perceived to be targeting and vilifying rugby in particular, this may exacerbate the sense of alienation felt by many white, particularly Afrikaner, South Africans in the face of the loss of privileged status for their language and culture and the controversy attending affirmative action policies in the new era.[16] The issue is therefore a sensitive one. In this respect, it is helpful that the rugby inquiry was preceded by an extensive, six month judicial inquiry into the affairs of soccer. The Pickard Commission resulted in the powerful head of the South African Football Association, 'Stix' Morewa, losing his job, and a major overhaul of the organisation as a whole. This intrusive and far-reaching intervention in the affairs of the 'sport of the majority' should help to dissipate charges that rugby is being victimised because of its historic associations with white culture and racism.

It remains to be seen whether the inquiry will precipitate significant structural reforms within the SARFU and its leading provincial affiliate unions, or whether such interference in rugby by the government will ultimately make white officials ever more recalcitrant. However, the precedent of the Pickard Commission suggests that a major blood-letting is possible, with the hand of anti-Luyt reformers in rugby significantly strengthened, though Luyt fought the government in court in 1998 leading to the calling of Mandela as a witness.

The case of rugby in South Africa: implications for the study of politics in sport

As we outlined in the first chapter, there has been a growing literature analysing the role of politics in sport and the role of sport in national and international politics. We have endeavoured to demonstrate how politics has played a significant role in the historical development of rugby in South Africa and how the cultural importance of rugby to the dominant group during the apartheid era led to its centrality in debates over the cultural isolation of South Africa. There are perhaps few places where a particular sport has been tied so closely to racially defined difference, national imagining and domestic and international politics as has been the case of rugby union in South Africa. Having said that, it is clear that many modern states and leaders have placed great emphasis on the importance of sport to both national and political prestige. The examples are numerous, from Trujillo's Dominican Republic, to Australia, Cuba, East Germany, the Soviet Union, New Zealand, Ireland and many others. What has made rugby in South Africa so striking is that it was crucial both in terms of domestic politics in the old *and* new South Africas, and in the international politics of sanctions debates and transnational anti-apartheid organisation. The combination of these factors make this story a valuable case study of the workings of politics within sport, domestic politics and sport, gendered politics and sport, transnational political organisation, sport and international relations and the increasingly global political economy of sport. We have tried to highlight elements of each of these areas within our analysis of the history and contemporary place of rugby in South African society and international relations.

It is clear that sport, more particularly specific sporting codes in different contexts, is a highly charged emotional arena that politicians and other political actors routinely seek to exploit in their attempts to connect with the national body politic. It is, in part, the perceived apolitical nature of sport that often makes it such a potent political tool as its full political meaning and significance is often obscured and its ramifications often escape critical scrutiny. Despite ideological constructs of the separation of politics and sport, however, it is clear that they have been tightly intertwined for most of the twentieth century and before. In South Africa, as our study demonstrates, rugby has been linked to the politics of racially divided cultural identities since the formation of the first clubs in the 1870s and 1880s. That it remained racially divided well past the time of desegregation of sport in most other societies made rugby in South Africa such a sensitive target for international sanctions. It also made the effort to negotiate non-racial unity and the renewal of international competition in the sport a prolonged and difficult process, with important precedent-setting implications for other, more central aspects of the transition.

Moreover, all indications are that while the racial politics of sport in South Africa have changed, politicians of all partisan persuasions continue to see sport as a dimension of national life worthy of their assiduous attention – as a potentially vital force in nation-building (or dividing), in establishing a new and more positive profile in international affairs, and in promoting national economic development through tourism in particular. Rugby's place in the South African sporting and political firmament is destined for a difficult period of adjustment and change, and a diminished status overall. But it will remain an important influence on, and bellweather for, the broader process of social and political change in the making of a new South Africa.

Notes

1 *SARFU's Official Guide to the 1997 Lions Tour* (Cape Town, SARFU, 1997), p. 30.
2 P. FitzSimons, *The Rugby War* (Sydney, HarperSports, 1996). This section is drawn from FitzSimons superbly detailed inside account of the events sur-

rounding the WRC attempts to start a new rugby union competition. It should be noted, however, that HarperSports is a division of HarperCollins owned by Murdoch's News Limited Corporation and FitzSimons is a presenter on *Fox Sports* in Australia. Nevertheless, FitzSimons is a shrewd and credible journalist with superb knowledge of the inner workings of rugby union. He makes it clear, for example, that he was on the side of the establishment at the time.

3 FitzSimons, *The Rugby War*, pp. 161–3.
4 Steve Morris, 'Making it easy for All Blacks', *Mail and Guardian* (Johannesburg), 18–24 July 1997.
5 A defensive strategy originating with the nineteenth-century trekkers, who would circle their ox wagons to protect themselves from hostile forces.
6 Donald McRae, 'Second phase is taking an age', *Mail and Guardian*, 27 June–3 July 1997.
7 'Too Luyt for the new order', *Mail and Guardian*, 1–7 November. 1996.
8 McRae, 'Second phase'.
9 *Mail and Guardian*, 27 June–3 July 1997.
10 'A nation of infidels', *Mail and Guardian* (electronic edition), 21 February 1997. Website: http://www.mg.co.za/mg.
11 Clinton van der Berg, 'Saving the soul of rugby', *Saturday Star* (Johannesburg), 27 September 1997.
12 E. Griffiths, *One Team, One Country: The Greatest Year of Springbok Rugby* (London, Viking Penguin, 1996).
13 'Louis Luyt profile', *Mail and Guardian* (electronic edition), 19 September 1996.
14 For an interesting discussion of Manuel's remarks see the 'The Springboks: symbol of unity or division?', *Mail and Guardian* (electronic edition), 14 August 1996.
15 R. Lascaris, 'Olympic bid highlights SA's failure to sell itself to a critical world', *Star* (Johannesburg), 27 September 1997. Lascaris is the joint chairperson of TBWA Hunt Lascaris Advertising.
16 *Globe and Mail* (Toronto), 31 October 1997.

Index

Note: 'n.' after a page number indicates a note on that page.

Scotland 25, 30–1, 34, 84, 150
Seddon, Richard 81
segregation 27, 40, 42, 47, 54, 56, 60
Serfontein, Hentie 149
Sharpeville 82, 121n.58
Shosholoza 124, 127, 131, 133,
    138n.8
Sivewright, Sir James 32
Skota, Mweli 46
Slack, Andrew 102
soccer 10, 14, 24, 39, 42–3, 47, 84,
    114, 148, 155
Soccer World Cup 128, 150, 152
South Africa New Zealand
    Australia Rugby Inc. 145
South African Amateur Athletic
    Association 26
South African Breweries 102
South African Broadcasting
    Corporation 147
South African College 30
South African Coloured Rugby
    Football Board 49, 55–6
South African Communist Party
    105, 114
South African Council of Sport 18,
    72–3, 84, 104–5
South African Cricket Association
    27
South African Cricket Union 105
South African Football Association
    155
South African Non-Racial Olympic
    Committee 55–6
South African Rugby Association
    109
South African Rugby Board 17, 27,
    31, 48, 55–6, 62, 64–5, 70, 74, 85,
    87, 100–4, 107–13
South African Rugby Football
    Federation 56, 70, 109
South African Rugby Football
    Union 109–13, 115, 117, 124,
    126–38, 143–9, 153, 155
South African Rugby Union 18, 56,
    72, 103–4, 107–12, 149
South African Sports Association
    55, 82

South African War 26, 28, 31, 33–4
South America 24, 65, 101
South Sea Barbarians 101
Soviet Union 4, 8, 155
Soweto 85, 121n.58, 147
Springboks 15, 25, 33–4, 39, 56, 62,
    64, 72, 77, 84, 86–7, 103, 110,
    113, 116–17, 122–5, 127, 131–2,
    135, 144–7, 150–4
St John's College 147
Stellenbosch 31, 34, 109
Stop the Seventy Tour Campaign 68
Stransky, Joel 153
Straueli, Rudolph 153
Strydom, Steve 108, 118n.6
Super 12 145–7, 153

television 82, 123–4, 137
Telkom Park 143
tennis 26, 42, 46
Thistles Rugby Club 49
Thompson, Richard 80
Tonks, Eddie 79, 109
Top Sport 118
Trafalgar High School 54
Transvaal 27, 32, 44, 69, 136, 147
Transvaal Rugby Football Union 86,
    112, 115, 117, 136, 144, 146, 148
Treaty of Waitangi 81
Treurnicht, Andries 70
Tri-Nations 146
Tshwete, Steve 11, 103, 107–9, 114,
    118, 119n.18, 143–4, 148, 154
Turnbull, Ross 102
Tutu, Desmond 124–5, 150
Twickenham 34
Tyamzashe, Mthobi 148

United Cricket Board of South
    Africa 106–7
United Democratic Front 14, 42
United Nations 83
United Party 82
United States of America 8, 35, 38
Universal Rugby Club 49
University of Cape Town 54
University of Potchefstroom 111
University of Pretoria 35